WRITE SOURCE

A Book for Writing, Thinking, and Learning

Written and Compiled by

**Dave Kemper, Patrick Sebranek,
and Verne Meyer**

Illustrated by

Chris Krenzke

WRITE SOURCE®

GREAT SOURCE EDUCATION GROUP

a division of Houghton Mifflin Company
Wilmington, Massachusetts

Reviewers

Genevieve Bodnar NBCT
Youngstown City Schools
Youngstown, Ohio

Mary M. Fischer
Arlington Public Schools
Arlington, Massachusetts

Cynthia Fontenot
Green T. Lindon Elementary
Lafayette, Louisiana

Heather Hagstrum
Unified School District #475
Ft. Riley, Kansas

Lisa Kickbusch
Pattonville School District
St. Ann, Missouri

Michele A. Lewis
Pattonville School District
St. Ann, Missouri

Joyce Martin
Forest Ridge
   Elementary School
Howard County
Laurel, Maryland

Kim T. Mickle
Alief Independent
   School District
Houston, Texas

Lisa D. Miller
Greater Clark County Schools
Jeffersonville, Indiana

Karen A. Reid
Rosemead School District
Rosemead, California

Roslyn Rowley-Penk
Renton School District
Renton, Washington

Jeannine M. Shirley, M. Ed.
White Hall School District
White Hall, Arkansas

Tanya Smith
Frankford Elementary School
Frankford, Delaware

Technology Connection for *Write Source*

Visit our Web site for additional student models, writing prompts,
multimedia reports, information about submitting your writing, and more.

The Write Source Web site . . . www.thewritesource.com

Printed in the United States of America

International Standard Book Number: 978-0-669-51804-7 (hardcover)

2 3 4 5 6 7 8 9 10 -RRDC- 11 10 09 08 07 06

International Standard Book Number: 978-0-669-51809-2 (softcover)

3 4 5 6 7 8 9 10 -RRDC- 11 10 09 08 07

Welcome to the *Write Source*!

This *Write Source* book was written just for you. We hope you have fun and learn, too.

Enjoy writing,

Your friends at the Write Source

Using the *Write Source* Book

Your *Write Source* book includes lessons and tips about writing. You will learn to write letters, reports, stories, poems, and more.

Besides writing, you will learn how to listen, speak, and take tests in class. Finally, a special section, called the "Proofreader's Guide," explains the rules of writing.

Contents

The Process of Writing

The Writing Process **2**

The Forms of Writing

Paragraph Writing 42

Descriptive Writing 50

Narrative Writing 62

Expository Writing 96

Persuasive Writing 130

Responding to Literature **162**

Speaking and Learning Skills 284

Words and Sentences 310

A Writer's Resource **350**

Proofreader's Guide **380**

Why Write?

The main reason to write is to communicate with others. Writing is an important way to share your feelings, thoughts, stories, and ideas.

Writing will help you . . .

- **share with others.** You can tell your friends and family all about you in letters, cards, notes, and e-mail messages.

- **remember more.** You can remember better when you write facts and ideas in your own words.

- **learn more about you.** You will discover your own thoughts and feelings by writing.

- **have fun.** You can imagine wonderful things in the stories, poems, and plays you write.

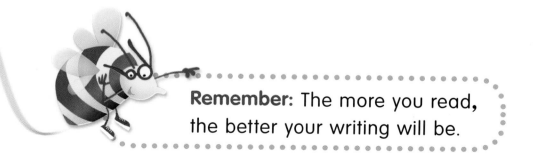

Remember: The more you read, the better your writing will be.

The Writing Process

There are many ways to get ready to write. Tim thinks quietly before he writes. Gina draws pictures about her story. José likes to talk about his ideas.

In this part of the *Write Source* book, you will follow the writing process from prewriting to sharing your finished story.

What's Ahead

- Using the Writing Process
- Studying One Writer's Process
- Working with a Partner
- Understanding the Writing Traits
- Connecting the Process and the Traits
- Using a Rubric
- Publishing and Portfolios

Using the
Writing Process

Would you like to be a great writer? It can happen! The more you write, the better your writing will be. In this chapter, you will learn to combine your imagination with the tools of writing.

Becoming a Writer

Here are four tools that all writers use.

Read   Reading wakes up your imagination. Read lots of stories, magazines, books, plays, and poems.

Practice   Write a lot. Practice writing notes, letters, stories, poems, and essays. Keep a writing journal.

Experience   Try new things. The more experiences you have, the more topics you can write about.

Observe   Writers look and listen. They pay attention to what they see, hear, taste, smell, and feel. Then they write about it.

Understanding the Writing Process

Here are the five steps of the writing process. Follow the steps whenever you have a writing assignment.

Prewrite

- **Choose** a topic that you like.
- **Gather** details about your topic.
- **Talk** with a partner about your writing ideas.

Write

- Write your **topic sentence**.
- Add details in the body sentences.
- Write your closing sentence.

Revise

- **Read** your writing to a classmate.
- **Look** for the traits of good writing.
- **Change** parts to make your writing better.

Edit

- **Check** your capitalization, punctuation, and spelling.
- **Check** one last time for mistakes.

Publish

- **Make** a neat final copy of your writing.
- **Share** your writing with others.
- **See** page **37** for other ideas.

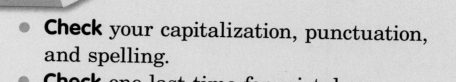

Whenever you see a pencil
in this book, it means it is time
to work on your writing.

Talk it over.

1. What kind of stories do you like to read?
2. What do you like to write about?

Studying
One Writer's Process

Monica's class had fun learning about holidays from around the world. Their teacher asked them to write a paragraph about one of the holidays.

Monica used the writing process to complete her paragraph. Follow along to see how Monica wrote about her topic.

Prewrite ▶ Choose a topic.

On the board, Monica's teacher listed holidays the class had studied. Monica decided to write about Children's Day, a special holiday in Japan.

Prewrite ▶ Gather your details.

Monica already knew something about her topic. She also read about it in library books. Then she drew pictures of the special details about Children's Day.

Monica's Pictures

Write ▶ Write a first draft.

Next, Monica wrote a paragraph about her topic. She included the ideas and details from her pictures. She will check her writing later.

Monica's First Draft

Children's Day

I lerned about Children's Day in school. It is a special day for the kids in Japan. They do fun stuff on this day. It comes on May 5. Children do not go to school on Children's Day they fly colorful fish kites from tall poles. They where paper hats and eat rice cakes. i think the fish kites would be fun to see. I wonder if rice cakes taste good.

Talk it over.

Which details in the pictures on page **9** did Monica use in her writing?

Revise ▶ Improve your writing.

Monica read her first draft aloud. Then she made changes to make her writing better.

An idea is cut, and a new idea is added.

An idea is moved.

New details are added.

Children's Day

I lerned about Children's Day in school. ~~Children have fun~~
It is a special day for the kids in Japan. ~~They~~
~~do fun stuff~~ on this day. (It comes on May 5.)

Children do not go to school on Children's

Day they fly colorful fish kites from tall poles.

wrapped in leaves
They where paper hats and eat rice cakes. ∧

i think the fish kites would be fun to see. I
and leaves
wonder if rice cakes taste good. ∧

Edit ▶ **Check for conventions.**

Next, Monica checked her writing for conventions. That means she corrected her capitalization, punctuation, and spelling.

A spelling mistake is fixed.	Children's Day
	learned I ⟨lerned⟩ about Children's Day in school. It comes on May 5. It is a special
A period and a capital letter are added.	day for the kids in Japan. Children have fun on this day. Children do not go to
	school on Children's Day. they fly colorful
A wrong word is fixed.	*wear* fish kites from tall poles. They ~~where~~ paper hats and eat rice cakes wrapped
	in leaves. i think the fish kites would be
A capital letter is added.	fun to see. I wonder if rice cakes and leaves taste good.

Publish ▶ Share your writing.

Finally, Monica made a neat copy of her writing and shared it with her teacher and class.

Monica's Paragraph

Children's Day

I learned about Children's Day in school. It comes on May 5. It is a special day for the kids in Japan. Children have fun on this day. Children do not go to school on Children's Day. They fly colorful fish kites from tall poles. They wear paper hats and eat rice cakes wrapped in leaves. I think the fish kites would be fun to see. I wonder if rice cakes and leaves taste good.

Working with a Partner

In art class, Luis made a coil pot. He was proud of his artwork and decided to write a story about it. When he shared his story with a partner, she gave him some good ideas. The ideas helped Luis make his writing even better. Now he is proud of his story, too.

Helping One Another

Here are some ways a partner can help you during the writing process.

Prewrite Partners can help you find topics and details.

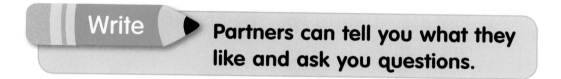

Write Partners can tell you what they like and ask you questions.

Revise Partners can tell you if your writing makes sense.

Edit Partners can help you check for conventions.

Publish Partners can enjoy your final copy.

Being on a Team

Working with a partner is like being on a team. One team member writes, and the other listens. Here are some tips to get you started.

When you are the writer
- Tell why you chose your topic.
- Read your writing to your partner.
- Pay attention to your partner's comments.

When you are the listener
- Look at your partner.
- Listen carefully to the story.
- Use a partner worksheet.
  1. Tell your partner what you like.
  2. Ask any questions you may have.

Using a Worksheet

Use a worksheet like the one below when you work with a partner.

Partner Worksheet

Writer _Luis_   Partner _Laura_

Title: _My Coil Pot_

1. One thing I like about your story

   I liked the way you told about
   making the long snake of clay.

2. One question I have about your story

   Who are you going to give the
   pot to?

Understanding the Writing Traits

You can use the *six traits* of writing listed below to become a better writer.

Ideas — Start with good ideas!

Organization — Make your writing easy to follow.

Voice — Sound as if you are talking to a friend.

Word Choice — Choose your words carefully.

Sentence Fluency — Use different lengths of sentences.

Conventions — Follow the rules for writing.

Ideas

Start with good ideas!

Alita likes writing about her family. She gathers details for her stories.

First, Alita thinks of a good **topic**.

Next, she lists **details** about her topic.

Writing topic

my baby sister

Details

- three months old
- cries when she is hungry
- wears pink and yellow
- smiles at me
- sleeps a lot
- looks like my baby pictures

Practice

1. Think of a topic you would like to write about.
2. In a writing notebook, write down your topic and at least three details about it.
3. Share your ideas with a partner.

Organization

Make your writing easy to follow.

Cole makes sure that his writing always has a beginning, a middle, and an ending.

My Sailing Adventure

Beginning

This part names the topic.

Last summer, I had an adventure with my grandma. We went to the harbor in Baltimore to sail on a tall ship.

Middle

The middle adds details.

First, we pulled on ropes to help put up the sails. Then we sailed out to sea. The ship moved up and down. Soon we couldn't even see land. Squawking seagulls flew around us. When the crew first fired the cannon, the noise and smoke scared me. Then I started laughing.

Ending

The ending shares a final thought.

Grandma and I had a great time. I can't wait for our next adventure.

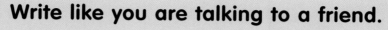

Voice

Write like you are talking to a friend.

Julian's writing voice sounds just like he is talking.

Julian uses contractions because that's how he talks.

I'm Julian, and my dog is my best buddy. Can you guess what his name is? That's right! It's Buddy.

Buddy eats strange things. He chews on rugs and bones. He likes liver. Once he even ate a raw fish. Wow, he smelled awful!

Words like *wow* show his feelings.

Buddy always spends time with me. Every morning, he walks me to the school bus. He's always waiting at the bus stop when I get home. At night, my best buddy sleeps on my bed.

Practice

Tell a partner a story about an animal. Then write the story. Does your writing sound like you are talking?

Word Choice ▶ **Choose your words carefully.**

> Riley uses words that make her writing clear.

General words (not clear)
> A boy came into the room.

Clear words
> Marcus tiptoed into the kitchen.

Sentence Fluency **Use different lengths of sentences.**

> Jackson makes sure to use short and long sentences.

Jackson's sentences
> Rover barked. He saw a rabbit and chased it across the yard.

Practice

Which of these sentences uses clear words?
> I went there yesterday.
> I walked to school yesterday.

Conventions

Follow the rules for writing.

Before Mia hands in her writing, she uses a checklist to edit her work.

Edit ▶ **Use a checklist.**

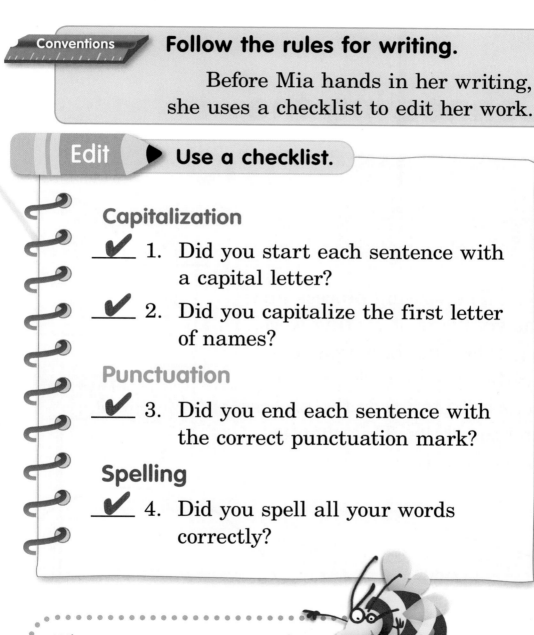

Capitalization

✔ 1. Did you start each sentence with a capital letter?

✔ 2. Did you capitalize the first letter of names?

Punctuation

✔ 3. Did you end each sentence with the correct punctuation mark?

Spelling

✔ 4. Did you spell all your words correctly?

Whenever you write, use the **six traits of good writing**.

Connecting the
Process and
the Traits

The writing process and the six traits of writing work together. Just like a garden needs the sun and the rain, your writing needs the process and the traits. This chapter shows how they connect.

Certain traits are important at each step in the writing process. The traits will help you improve your writing.

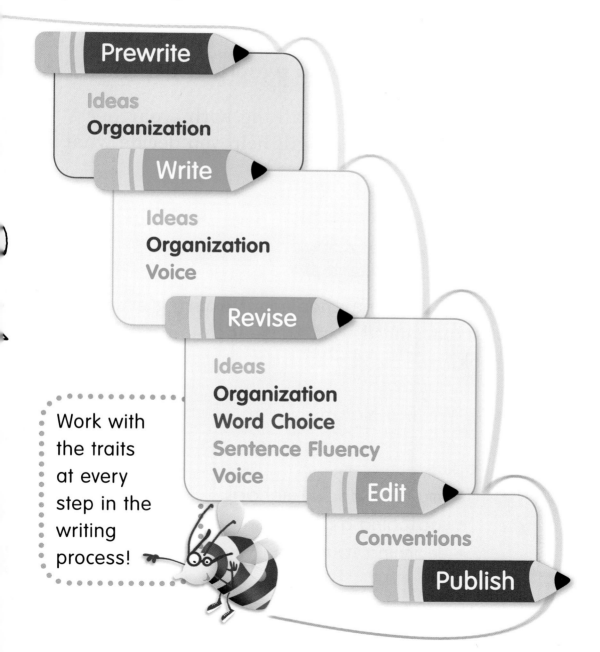

Prewrite

Ideas
Organization

Write

Ideas
Organization
Voice

Revise

Ideas
Organization
Word Choice
Sentence Fluency
Voice

Edit

Conventions

Publish

Work with the traits at every step in the writing process!

Connecting the Process and the Traits

To do your best writing, always connect the traits to each step in your writing process.

Prewrite ▶ **Choose a topic.**

Ideas

Reading, listing, and talking with a partner about different topic ideas will help you decide what to write about.

Talk it over.

Talk with a partner about exciting events you've experienced. List these ideas in a notebook.

Sample Writing Notebook

Topics
- my first day at school
- catching a giant fish
- learning to ride my bike

Prewrite ▶ **Sort your details.** Organization

After choosing a topic, it's time to write down all the details you know about it. You can put the details in order or sort them into groups by using an organizing tool. Here are two ways to organize your details.

Time Line

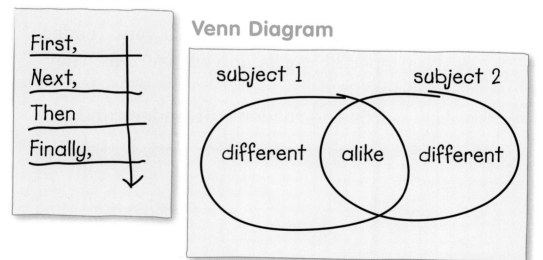

First,

Next,

Then

Finally,

Venn Diagram

subject 1   subject 2

different   alike   different

Practice

Choose a story idea from your writing notebook. Put the details of your story in order by using one of the tools on this page.

Write ▶ **Create your first draft.** Voice

When you write your story, make it sound as if you are talking to a friend. Your writing voice should sound like YOU!

Tips for finding the right voice:

- Think of your reader. Who will read your writing?
- Imagine yourself speaking to your reader.
- What special words do you use? Are they friendly?
- Use words the reader will understand.

Revise ▶ **Improve your writing.**

When you revise your first draft, you make your ideas, organization, and voice even better. Two ways to improve your writing are to check your word choice and your sentences.

 Change general words to clear words.

Use **tiger** instead of *big cat.*
Use **hamburger** instead of *sandwich.*
Use **whisper** instead of *talk.*

 Write sentences that make sense and sound smooth.

Choppy: Jake went to the zoo. Jake saw the big cats. Jake liked the tiger best.

Smooth: Jake went to the zoo. He saw the big cats and liked the tiger best.

Edit ▶ **Check for conventions.** Conventions

Editing means checking that you have followed the rules of capitalization, punctuation, and spelling. These rules are called **conventions**.

You can use special symbols, or marks, as you revise and edit your writing:

 To cut a word from your writing, cross it out with a line and a loop.

> My dog Rex ~~he~~ is big.
>
> My dog Rex is big.

∧ To add a word, use a caret.

> meaty
> Rex likes his ∧ bone.
>
> Rex likes his meaty bone.

≡ This symbol tells you to capitalize a letter.

> i went to town.
> ≡
> I went to town.

/ This symbol tells you to make a letter lowercase.

> My /Mom ran.
> My mom ran.

◯ Circle words that you think may be spelled wrong.

> Joe is my (freind.)
> Joe is my friend.

 This symbol tells you to use a period.

> Tom likes to fish⊙
> Tom likes to fish.

Using a
Rubric

Hana loves to look at the rabbits at the county fair. Some of them get blue ribbons, and others get red or white ribbons. The different colors show how the judges scored each rabbit.

Your writing may be scored, too, with a scoring chart called a **rubric**. This chapter will explain how a rubric can help you.

Getting Started with a Rubric

At the beginning of some chapters in this book, you will see a chart like the one below. It will show the different traits of good writing. Your goals for the writing assignment will be listed.

Look at the goals for expository writing below. You may have these goals when you write a classroom science report.

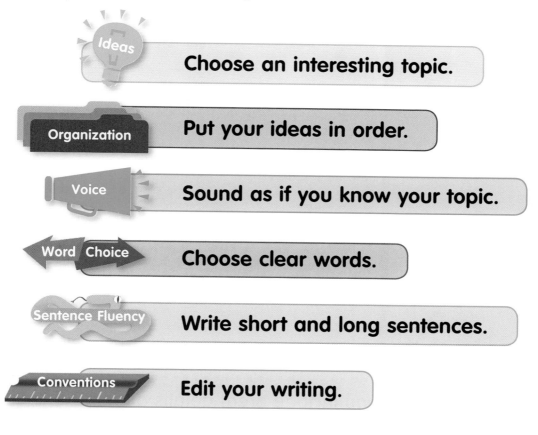

Ideas — Choose an interesting topic.

Organization — Put your ideas in order.

Voice — Sound as if you know your topic.

Word Choice — Choose clear words.

Sentence Fluency — Write short and long sentences.

Conventions — Edit your writing.

Understanding a Rubric

The information under each number in the rubric below can help you improve your writing. Each trait of writing can be scored.

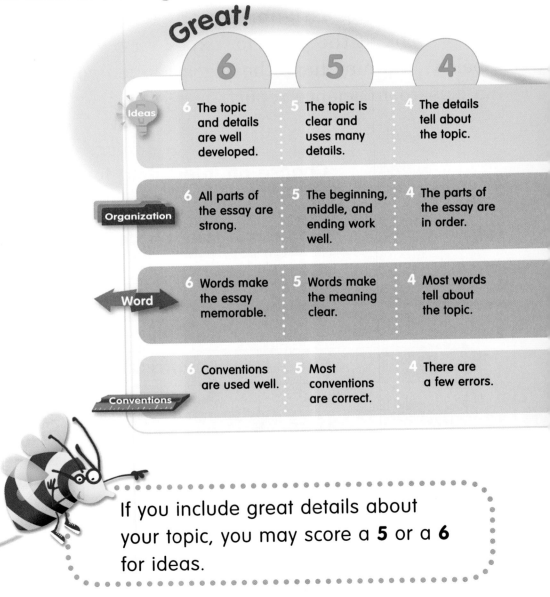

Great!

	6	5	4
Ideas	The topic and details are well developed.	The topic is clear and uses many details.	The details tell about the topic.
Organization	All parts of the essay are strong.	The beginning, middle, and ending work well.	The parts of the essay are in order.
Word	Words make the essay memorable.	Words make the meaning clear.	Most words tell about the topic.
Conventions	Conventions are used well.	Most conventions are correct.	There are a few errors.

If you include great details about your topic, you may score a **5** or a **6** for ideas.

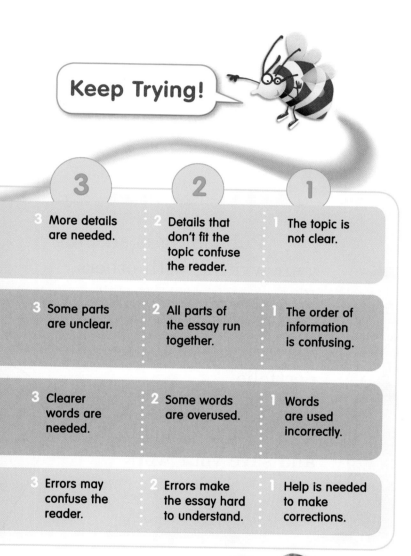

Keep Trying!

3	2	1
3 More details are needed.	**2** Details that don't fit the topic confuse the reader.	**1** The topic is not clear.
3 Some parts are unclear.	**2** All parts of the essay run together.	**1** The order of information is confusing.
3 Clearer words are needed.	**2** Some words are overused.	**1** Words are used incorrectly.
3 Errors may confuse the reader.	**2** Errors make the essay hard to understand.	**1** Help is needed to make corrections.

Talk it over.

1. Which traits are shown on this rubric?
2. Look at the ideas trait. How could you improve the ideas in your writing?

Publishing and Portfolios

Publishing is sharing your writing with others. Kara reads her story to her class. Denzel puts his writing in a showcase portfolio.

This chapter tells about ways to publish and save your work.

Finding Ideas for Publishing

Print it!
Make a book.

Act it out!
Act out your story for a class, your family, or friends.

Submit it!
Send your story to magazines that publish student writing.

Editor

Send it!
Write an e-mail.

Dear Auntie,
Here's my story.
Hope you like it.

Talk it over.

1. Which publishing idea would you like to try?
2. What other ways can you think of to share your writing?

Making a Neat Final Copy

Be very neat when you write your final copy. This shows that you care about your writing. It also makes your writing easy to read.

Handwritten Copy

Saturday

Saturday is the best day of the week. My family and I have breakfast together. Sometimes we have pancakes. Other times we have breakfast burritos. Then we might go grocery shopping. Some Saturdays we go to the park to kick a ball around. It doesn't matter where we go. We get to spend the day together. I love Saturdays!

Use one side of the paper.

Use your best penmanship.

Draw a picture.

Using a Computer

Follow this plan when you use a computer to make your final copy.

Computer Copy

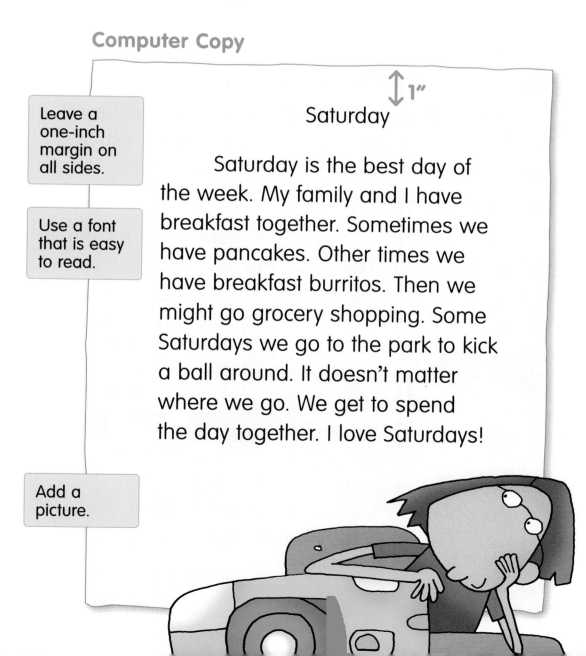

1"

Leave a one-inch margin on all sides.

Use a font that is easy to read.

Add a picture.

Saturday

Saturday is the best day of the week. My family and I have breakfast together. Sometimes we have pancakes. Other times we have breakfast burritos. Then we might go grocery shopping. Some Saturdays we go to the park to kick a ball around. It doesn't matter where we go. We get to spend the day together. I love Saturdays!

Understanding Portfolios

Leila keeps her rock collection in a special box. She keeps her finished stories in a portfolio. A **portfolio** is a special place to collect your writing. Here are two kinds of classroom portfolios.

Showcase Portfolio

In a *showcase portfolio,* you keep your best writing. Your teacher will help you decide which writing to include.

Growth Portfolio

In a *growth portfolio,* you save writing from different times of the year. You will be surprised how your writing improves.

You can use an electronic file on the computer for your portfolio.

You can use a special folder for your portfolio.

Making Your Own Portfolio

You can also make your own portfolio. You may want to save all kinds of things. Here are some ideas.

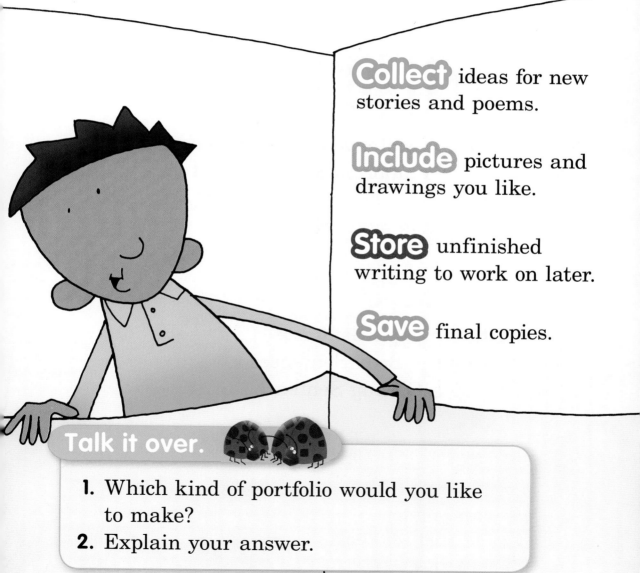

Collect ideas for new stories and poems.

Include pictures and drawings you like.

Store unfinished writing to work on later.

Save final copies.

Talk it over.

1. Which kind of portfolio would you like to make?
2. Explain your answer.

Paragraph Writing

When you write, you can describe something awesome or give information. You can tell how to do something or share an interesting story. You can do all of these things by writing a paragraph.

What's Ahead

- Writing a Topic Sentence
- Writing the Body Sentences
- Writing a Closing Sentence

Writing a
Paragraph

Theo wanted to describe something special that he saw. He wrote a paragraph about it. A **paragraph** is a group of sentences about the same subject or topic. Look at the parts of Theo's paragraph.

Today:
PARAGRAPH

101

Theo's Paragraph

What I Saw

Topic Sentence

   I saw a big hot-air balloon that looked like my sister's knee socks. It had bright blue and yellow stripes. A big basket hung under the balloon with a man inside it. The man shot

Body Sentences

spurts of fire into the balloon as it passed over my head. Whoosh, whoosh! The flames made a loud sound. I waved to the man, and he waved back! It was the coolest

Closing Sentence

thing I have ever seen.

- The **topic sentence** tells what the paragraph is about. It states the main idea.
- The **body sentences** describe the topic.
- The **closing sentence** adds one last thought.

Writing Create a topic sentence.

A topic sentence names the main idea or topic of the paragraph. Theo wrote his topic sentence in two different ways. Then he chose the one he liked best.

Ask a question.

Have you ever seen a hot-air balloon?

Make a comparison.

I saw a hot-air balloon that looked like my sister's knee socks.

Talk it over.

Do you like Theo's choice? Tell why or why not.

Indent each paragraph.

You **indent** a paragraph because it starts a new idea. *Indenting* means to begin a line farther in from the margin.

Example

> The lion came close to the edge of its cage. It looked right at me. The lion growled, "Grrr!"
>
> Suddenly, Dad called me.

Talk it over.

Look at the writing below. What is the new idea in the second paragraph?

Guess what. I learned to swim! At first I was afraid of the water. Soon I was brave enough to swim in deep water. Now swimming is my favorite thing to do.

My little brother is learning to swim. I am helping him, but he is still a little afraid of the water. Today we will go swimming. I like swimming with my brother.

Writing **Put the sentences in order.**

The body sentences of a paragraph include clear details listed in a **logical order**. Here are two ways to organize a paragraph.

Time Order

Time order shows details in the order in which they happened. It helps the reader understand what happened from start to finish.

Place Order

Place order shows details in the order in which you see them. You may describe them from top to bottom or from left to right. It helps the reader see what something looks like.

Time Order Words		Place Order Words	
first	soon	above	near
next	now	below	into
then	when	on top of	inside
before long		through	

Writing Add a closing sentence.

A closing sentence gives one more detail and ends the paragraph. Theo wrote his closing sentence in two different ways. Then he chose the one he liked best.

Restate the main idea.

Seeing the hot-air balloon was fun.

Add a final thought.

It was the coolest thing I have ever seen.

Talk it over.

Can you think of another closing sentence for Theo's paragraph?

Descriptive Writing

In descriptive writing, you tell about people, places, or things that you know about. You include details you can see, hear, smell, taste, or touch. They create pictures in your reader's mind and make your writing fun to read!

What's Ahead

- Writing a Descriptive Paragraph
- Writing Across the Curriculum

Writing a
Descriptive Paragraph

Isabel described her friend Marty in a descriptive paragraph. In a way, she painted a picture with words. You can make a *word picture* of someone you know, too! This chapter will show you how.

Isabel's Paragraph

My Teammate Marty

Topic Sentence

My friend Marty is on my soccer team. He wears a blue baseball cap. His hair is dark brown. His

Body Sentences

eyes light up when he smiles. Marty smiles a lot. He likes red T-shirts, blue pants, and white shoes. His shoes wear out quickly. That's because Marty loves playing

Closing Sentence

soccer. He runs fast and plays fair. Marty is a great teammate.

- The **topic sentence** tells who the paragraph is about.
- The body sentences describe what the person looks like and what he or she does.
- The closing sentence tells how the writer feels about the person.

Prewriting Choose a topic.

After Isabel decided to write about Marty, she drew a picture of him. Her drawing helped her remember details.

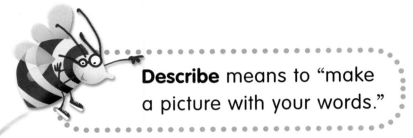

Describe means to "make a picture with your words."

Prewrite ▶ Choose a topic.

1. Think of people you know well and could describe.
2. List the names of at least three people.
3. Choose one person to describe in your paragraph. Circle the name.
4. Draw a picture of the person.

Gather your details.

Isabel made a list of details about her topic. She picked words that made a picture in her mind.

Sensory details tell what you see, hear, smell, taste, or touch. Isabel chose two kinds of sensory details for her list. She also wrote down things she knew about the person.

Details List

Topic: Marty

See	Hear	Know About
brown eyes	soft voice	on my team
baseball cap	squeaky shoes	loves soccer
red T-shirt		plays hard
blue pants		worn-out shoes
big smile		lives next door
dark brown hair		likes popcorn

Prewrite ▶ **Create a details list.**

1. Make a list about your person.
2. Write about what you see, hear, and know.

Writing Create your paragraph.

Each part of your paragraph has a special job.
(See page **53**.)

Write ▶ **Write your first draft.**

1. Write your **topic sentence**. Your topic
   sentence should tell who you are writing
   about. Write your own sentence or use the
   form below.

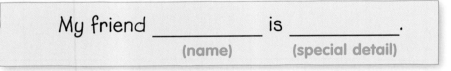

> My friend _____ is _____.
> (name)   (special detail)

2. Write your body sentences. The body
   sentences should describe the person.
   Choose words and details from your list.

3. Write your closing sentence. In your closing
   sentence, tell how you feel about the person.

My Teammate Marty

My friend Marty is on my soccer
team. He wears a blue baseball
cap. His hair is dark brown. His
eyes light up when he smiles. Marty
smiles a lot. He likes red T-shirts,
blue pants, and white shoes. His
shoes wear out quickly. That's
because Marty loves playing
soccer. He runs fast and plays fair.
Marty is a great teammate.

Revising and Editing

Now it's time to make your descriptive paragraph even better. Use the questions below to make changes and correct your writing.

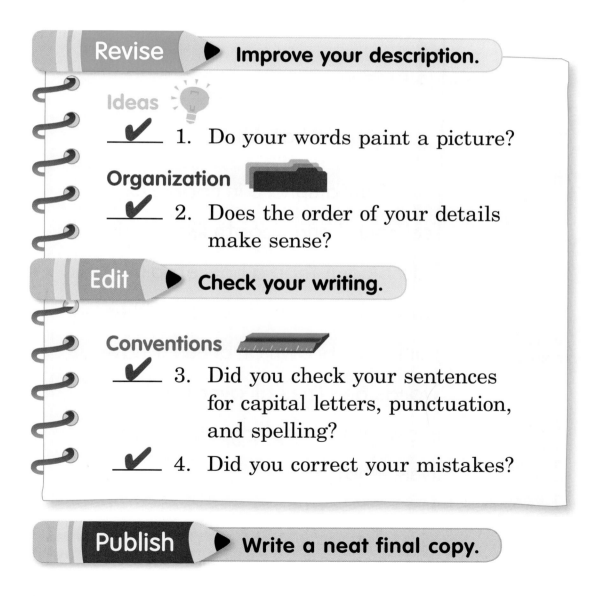

Revise ▶ **Improve your description.**

Ideas

✔ 1. Do your words paint a picture?

Organization

✔ 2. Does the order of your details make sense?

Edit ▶ **Check your writing.**

Conventions

✔ 3. Did you check your sentences for capital letters, punctuation, and spelling?

✔ 4. Did you correct your mistakes?

Publish ▶ **Write a neat final copy.**

Across the Curriculum

Science or Math: A Shape Riddle

In science or math class, you may be asked to write about a shape. Ronnie wrote this riddle for his science class.

Ronnie's Shape Riddle

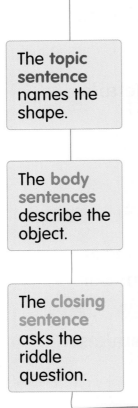

The **topic sentence** names the shape.

The **body sentences** describe the object.

The **closing sentence** asks the riddle question.

What Am I?

I am a sphere in room 213. I feel round and smooth like a ball. I am bigger than a basketball. Some parts of me are blue. Other parts are brown or green. I have words and lines all over me. I can show you where anyone on Earth lives. What am I?

Answer: a globe

Writing Tips

Before You Write

- Pick an object in your classroom that has a special shape.
- Write the headings from the sensory list that fit your topic.
- List words for each heading.

Sensory List

see	
hear	
smell	
taste	
feel	

During Your Writing

- Name your object's shape in the **topic sentence**.
- Include details from your list in the body sentences.
- In the closing sentence, write your riddle question.

After You Write

- Read your riddle to a partner to see if it makes sense.
- Add or change details to make your riddle clear.
- Correct mistakes and make a final copy.

Across the Curriculum

Practical Writing: An E-Mail

Sending e-mail is fun. Paul wrote to his friend Jo about a park near his home in Florida.

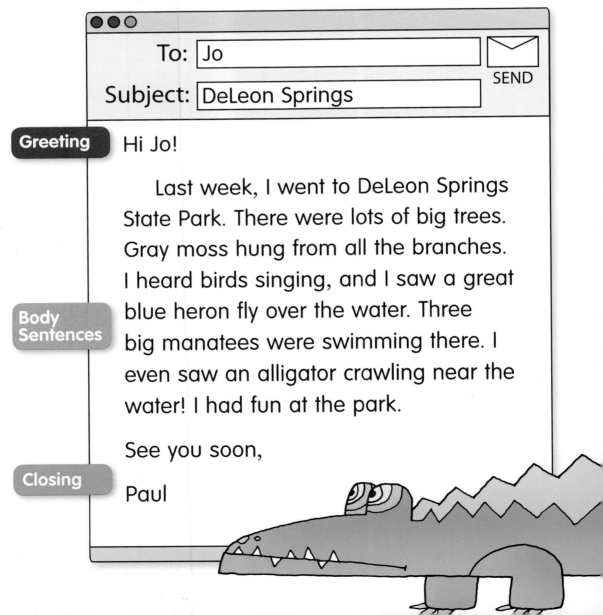

To: Jo

Subject: DeLeon Springs

SEND

Greeting

Hi Jo!

Body Sentences

Last week, I went to DeLeon Springs State Park. There were lots of big trees. Gray moss hung from all the branches. I heard birds singing, and I saw a great blue heron fly over the water. Three big manatees were swimming there. I even saw an alligator crawling near the water! I had fun at the park.

See you soon,

Closing

Paul

▶ **Writing Tips**

Before You Write

- Choose a person to receive your e-mail.
- Pick a place to describe.
- Make a sensory list to gather details about the place.

Sensory List

See	
Hear	
Smell	
Taste	
Feel	

During Your Writing

- Begin with a fun **greeting**.
- Share ideas from your list in the **body sentences**.
- Make your **closing** a friendly good-bye.

After You Write

- Read over your e-mail. Be sure you have clearly described a place.
- Correct mistakes in capitalization, punctuation, and spelling.
- Send your final e-mail to the person you chose and to your teacher.

Narrative Writing

You're always telling stories about what happens to you, right? When you write those stories down, they're called narratives. In a narrative, you can tell what happened when you were five or what just happened last Tuesday. This section will help you write narratives.

What's Ahead

- Writing a Narrative Paragraph
- Writing a Narrative Essay
- Writing Across the Curriculum
- Writing for Assessment

Writing a
Narrative
Paragraph

The students in Colin's class talked about special times they remembered. They discovered many stories to tell about themselves, their families, and their friends.

Colin decided to write about a visit to the zoo. In this chapter, you will write a paragraph about a special experience you've had.

Colin's Paragraph

My Zoo Surprise

Topic Sentence

   My big brother and I had an amazing time at the zoo. The peacocks squawked and fanned out their tails. Prairie dogs chased each other and dived into their burrows. Then my brother told me he would show me his favorite animal.

Body Sentences

We squeezed through the crowd to get to a huge window where you could see underwater. Suddenly a polar bear crashed into the water in front of us. It pushed its nose right up to the window!

Closing Sentence

Everybody screamed! My big brother and I were nose to nose with a polar bear!

- The **topic sentence** tells the main idea of the paragraph.
- The **body sentences** tell what happened.
- The **closing sentence** gives the reader something to think about.

Prewriting Choose a topic.

Colin's teacher wrote a list of places where children often have special times. Colin chose to write about his trip to the zoo.

Places List

kitchen	*zoo	park
playground	farm	pool
grandma's house	bike trail	museum

Prewrite ▶ **Choose your topic.**

1. List places where you've had special times.
2. Choose a place and a time to write about.

Gather details.

To gather details for his story, Colin made a chart. He listed events in the order they happened. (This is called *time order*.) Then he told how he felt about what happened.

Events	How I Felt
1. One day I went to the zoo with my big brother.	
2. We saw peacocks and prairie dogs.	excited
3. A polar bear jumped into the water.	
4. He pushed his nose up to the window.	surprised
5. We screamed.	happy

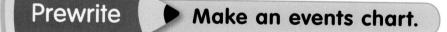

Prewrite ▶ **Make an events chart.**

1. Make a chart like the one above.
2. List the events of your story in time order.
3. Then tell how you felt.

Writing Create your first draft.

Each part of your paragraph has a different job.

Write ▶ **Start your first draft.**

1. First, write your **topic sentence**. Tell the main idea of your story. If you need help getting started, fill in the sentence form below on your paper.

> I had an amazing time with _____
> (person)
>
> at the _____ .
> (place)

2. Next, write the body sentences using the ideas from your events chart (page **67**). Write as if you are talking to a friend.

3. Finally, in the closing sentence, leave the reader with something to think about.

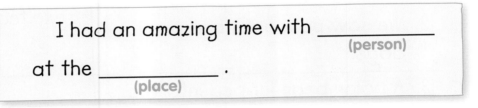

Revising and Editing

After Colin finished his first draft, he changed some parts. Use the checklist below to make your essay better.

Revise ▶ **Improve your story.**

Organization

✔ ___ 1. Did you put the events of your story in the right order?

Voice

✔ ___ 2. Does your story sound as if you're telling it to a friend?

Edit ▶ **Check your writing.**

Conventions

✔ ___ 3. Did you use capital letters and punctuation correctly?

✔ ___ 4. Did you spell words correctly?

Publish ▶ **Share your work.**

Print a neat copy and add a drawing.

Writing a
Narrative Essay

Fred helps his grandpa in a community garden. He writes stories to tell about his adventures! A narrative essay uses more than one paragraph to tell about a true experience.

Goals for Writing

The traits below will help you write a narrative essay.

Ideas **Tell about one special experience.**

Organization **List what happened in order from first to last.**

Voice **Write as if you are talking to a friend. This is called your writer's voice.**

Conventions **Check your writing for correct use of capital letters, punctuation, and spelling.**

Fred's Narrative Essay

My Day at the Community Garden

Beginning

I remember when Grandpa took me to the community garden. We only had to walk one block. Lots of neighbors were there, too. I saw rows and rows of plants!

Middle

Grandpa showed me lettuce, beets, peas, and corn. Then he showed me how to pull weeds without pulling the vegetables. It's not easy. He told me that garden work is important. He said, "People who have food need to share it." Finally, we took the food from the garden to a shelter. I felt proud working with Grandpa. He told me I was his big helper.

Ending

Now I know about growing vegetables and pulling weeds. The best part was spending time with Grandpa. I learned that working together and helping others is fun.

Parts of an Essay

Fred wrote about a garden in his grandfather's city. He tells about his time with his grandfather in the garden. Look at the parts of his essay.

Beginning   In the first paragraph, Fred tells where the story took place.

Middle   In the second paragraph, Fred writes about his day with his grandfather.

Ending   In the last paragraph, Fred explains what he learned and how he feels.

After You Read

- **Ideas** (1) What experience did Fred tell about?
- **Organization** (2) What order did Fred use to tell about his day with his grandfather?
- **Voice** (3) Find a sentence that tells how Fred felt.

Prewriting **Choose a topic.**

Kelsey's class talked about special times with their families. Then Kelsey made a list of places she had been.

Kelsey thought about each place. She decided to write about a special event that happened at Standing Rock. Kelsey circled her choice.

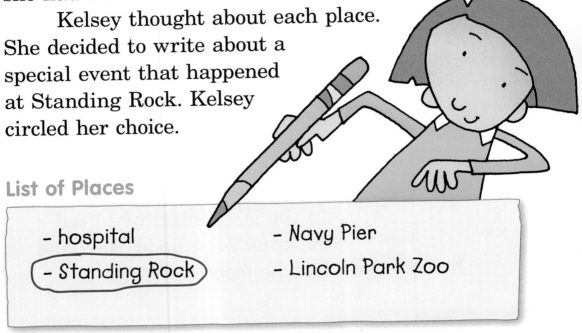

List of Places

- hospital
- Standing Rock
- Navy Pier
- Lincoln Park Zoo

Prewrite ▶ **Make a list.**

1. Make a list of places that you have visited. Has something special happened to you in one of these places?
2. Circle that place and plan to write about it.

Gather details.

Kelsey made a chart about the setting of her story. Then she gathered more ideas and details for her story by making a cluster.

Setting Chart

When?	Where?
one summer	Standing Rock

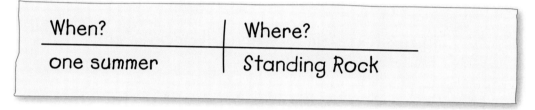

• List when and where your story takes place.

Ideas Cluster

1. Write the main thing that happened.
2. Add details around it.

Writing **Begin your story.**

Beginning

Middle

Ending

You can start a narrative in more than one way. Here are two ways you can write a beginning sentence.

Describe *where* the story takes place.

> Huge stone cliffs were all around us.

Answer *when, who,* and *what* for the story.

> One Saturday, my family and my cousins went to Standing Rock state park.

Kelsey wrote her beginning sentence. She tried two ways to start her paragraph.

> I had a fun time one summer.
>
> One summer my family and I went to Standing Rock state park.

Kelsey decided that the second choice was better. It used clearer words.

Kelsey's Beginning Paragraph

Here is Kelsey's beginning paragraph. She left space between the lines so that she could make corrections later.

The **beginning** introduces the experience and the setting.

> One summer, my family and I went to Standing Rock state park. We walked on trails through stone cliffs. Waterfalls fell over high rocks I saw fuzzy green stuff on the edge of the path. Then I saw something really exciting!

Write ▶ Create your first paragraph.

1. Write your beginning paragraph. Tell where and when your story took place and who you were with.
2. Then describe the place.

Writing Create the middle.

One way to add interest to a narrative is to add dialogue. People in the story can speak. Dialogue adds voice and makes your story more interesting. Kelsey thought of dialogue she could use in her story.

Beginning

Middle

Ending

I said, "There's a baby raccoon here!"

Mom said, "It's too hot for anything to be alive in there."

" " Quotation marks show that someone is talking.

Kelsey's Middle Paragraph

Kelsey used the details from her ideas cluster to write her middle paragraph.

> Inside the garbage can, I found a raccoon. It was a small one. There's a baby raccoon here! I yelled. Dad and Mom told me they would look later. I was mad. No one beleved me. Who cared about seeing another waterfall? I wanted to help the little raccoon!

 Write ▶ **Create your middle paragraph.**

1. Look over your ideas cluster (page **75**).
2. Write the events in the order they happened.
3. Write about how you felt.
4. Include a quotation to add voice.

Writing **Complete your ending.**

One way to end your narrative is to share something you learned from your experience. Kelsey thought she learned about herself.

Beginning

Middle

Ending

Share something about yourself.

I could be a hero.

Share something about another person.

Park workers have an important job.

Share something about nature.

Wild animals like to be free.

Kelsey's Ending Paragraph

Kelsey decided to add the idea of being a hero to the end of her essay.

We finally got back from hiking. Dad looked in the garbage can and saw my raccoon! Then he found a park worker. She tipped the can over and the raccoon hurried into the woods. I learned that I could be a hero!

Write ▶ **Write your last paragraph.**

Think about what you learned from your experience.

1. Finish telling your story.
2. Write what you learned.

Revising Improve your writing.

After finishing your first draft, it's time to revise. Read over your essay and use the checklist below.

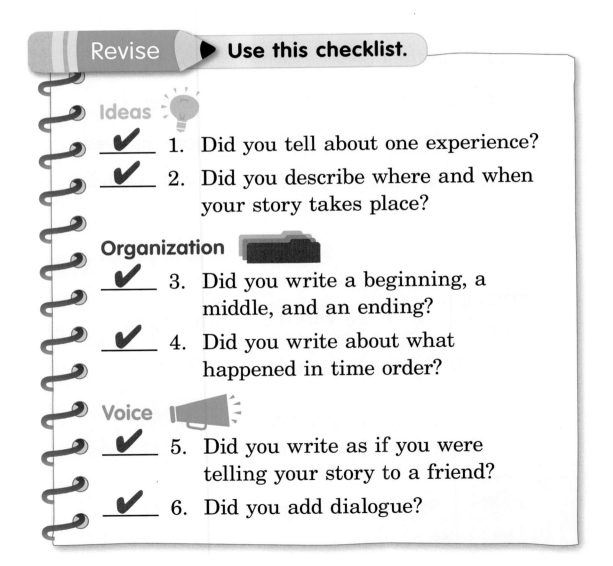

Revise ▶ **Use this checklist.**

Ideas

✔ 1. Did you tell about one experience?

✔ 2. Did you describe where and when your story takes place?

Organization

✔ 3. Did you write a beginning, a middle, and an ending?

✔ 4. Did you write about what happened in time order?

Voice

✔ 5. Did you write as if you were telling your story to a friend?

✔ 6. Did you add dialogue?

Kelsey's Revising

Kelsey revised her essay. The side notes tell you about the changes she made.

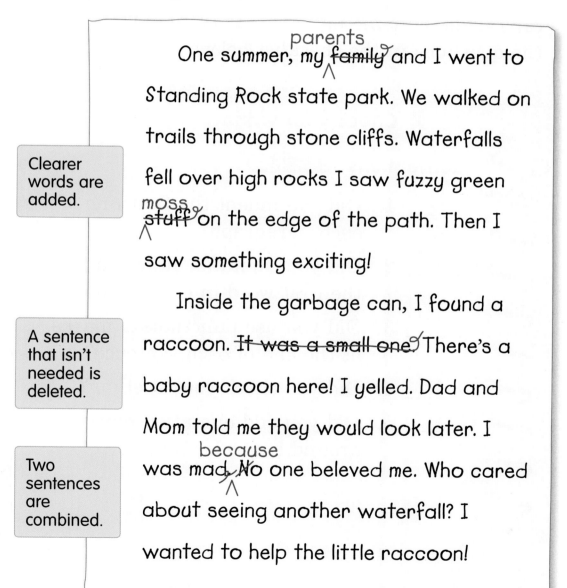

Clearer words are added.

One summer, my ~~family~~ parents and I went to Standing Rock state park. We walked on trails through stone cliffs. Waterfalls fell over high rocks I saw fuzzy green ~~stuff~~ moss on the edge of the path. Then I saw something exciting!

A sentence that isn't needed is deleted.

Inside the garbage can, I found a raccoon. ~~It was a small one.~~ There's a baby raccoon here! I yelled. Dad and Mom told me they would look later. I

Two sentences are combined.

was mad. No one beleved me. because Who cared about seeing another waterfall? I wanted to help the little raccoon!

Editing Check your writing.

Read over your revised essay carefully. It's time to check your writing for errors in capitalization, punctuation, and spelling. Use the questions in the checklist below.

Edit ▶ **Check your writing.**

Conventions

✔ 1. Did you indent the first line of each paragraph?

✔ 2. Did you capitalize names and the first word in each sentence?

✔ 3. Did you use punctuation marks at the end of each sentence?

✔ 4. Did you check your spelling?

✔ 5. Did you add quotation marks around a speaker's words?

Kelsey's Editing

Kelsey edited her paragraph for conventions.

Words that name a special place capitalized.

A period is added.

Quotation marks are put around the speaker's words.

A spelling mistake is corrected.

One summer, my parents and I went to Standing Rock state park. We walked on trails through stone cliffs. Waterfalls fell over high rocks. I saw fuzzy green moss on the edge of the path. Then I saw something exciting!

Inside the garbage can, I found a raccoon. "There's a baby raccoon here!" I yelled. Dad and Mom told me they would look later. I was mad because no one believed me. Who cared about seeing another waterfall? I wanted to help the little raccoon!

Publishing Finish your essay.

Standing Rock State Park

One summer, my parents and I went to Standing Rock State Park. We walked on trails through stone cliffs. Waterfalls fell over high rocks. I saw fuzzy green moss on the edge of the path. Then I saw something exciting!

Inside the garbage can, I found a raccoon. "There's a baby raccoon here!" I yelled. Dad and Mom told me they would look later. I was mad because no one believed me. Who cared about seeing another waterfall? I wanted to help the little raccoon!

We finally got back from hiking. Dad looked in the garbage can and saw my raccoon! Then Dad found a park ranger. She tipped the can over, and the raccoon hurried into the woods. I learned that I could be a hero!

Reflect on your writing.

After your essay is finished, take some time to think about your writing.

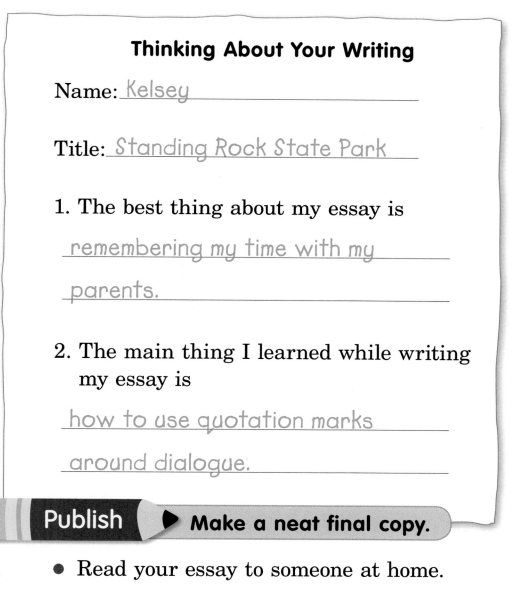

Thinking About Your Writing

Name: _Kelsey_

Title: _Standing Rock State Park_

1. The best thing about my essay is

   remembering my time with my

   parents.

2. The main thing I learned while writing my essay is

   how to use quotation marks

   around dialogue.

Publish ▶ **Make a neat final copy.**

● Read your essay to someone at home.

Using a Rubric

Great!

	6	5	4
Ideas	6 Rich details make an outstanding essay.	5 The essay shares one experience with rich details.	4 One experience is shared with some details.
Organization	6 The narrative is arranged wonderfully.	5 The experience is written in time order.	4 Most of the essay is in time order.
Voice	6 The voice is exciting and original.	5 The voice sounds just like the writer.	4 In most parts, the voice sounds like the writer.
Conventions	6 Conventions are correct.	5 Most conventions are correct.	4 There are a few errors.

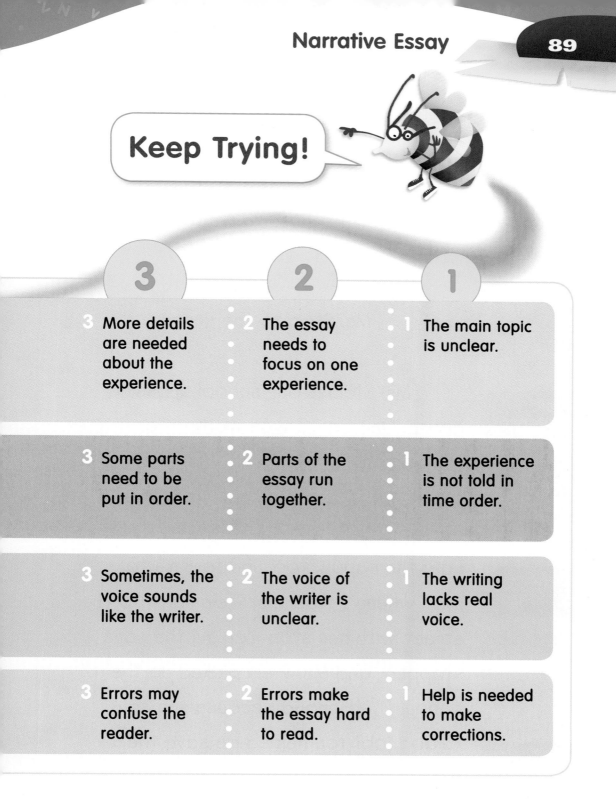

Keep Trying!

3

2

1

3 More details are needed about the experience.

2 The essay needs to focus on one experience.

1 The main topic is unclear.

3 Some parts need to be put in order.

2 Parts of the essay run together.

1 The experience is not told in time order.

3 Sometimes, the voice sounds like the writer.

2 The voice of the writer is unclear.

1 The writing lacks real voice.

3 Errors may confuse the reader.

2 Errors make the essay hard to read.

1 Help is needed to make corrections.

Across the Curriculum

Social Studies: A Community Helper

For social studies, Josie wrote a story about a community helper. She chose to write about a crossing guard.

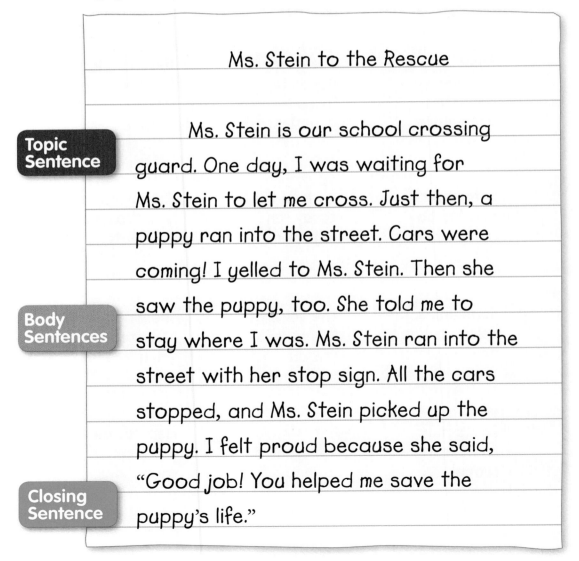

Ms. Stein to the Rescue

Topic Sentence

Ms. Stein is our school crossing guard. One day, I was waiting for Ms. Stein to let me cross. Just then, a puppy ran into the street. Cars were coming! I yelled to Ms. Stein. Then she saw the puppy, too. She told me to

Body Sentences

stay where I was. Ms. Stein ran into the street with her stop sign. All the cars stopped, and Ms. Stein picked up the puppy. I felt proud because she said, "Good job! You helped me save the

Closing Sentence

puppy's life."

▶ Writing Tips

Before You Write

- Make a list of community helpers.
- Think about an experience you shared with one of them.
- Use a time line to gather details about the experience.

Time Line

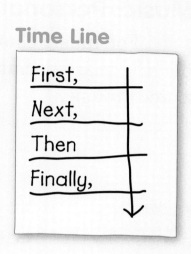

First,

Next,

Then

Finally,

During Your Writing

- In the **topic sentence**, name the person. Tell what kind of helper this person is.
- In the body of your paragraph, tell about the experience. Show what happened.
- In the closing sentence, tell why the experience was important to you.

After You Write

- Make sure you have included all the important details.
- Check your capitalization and punctuation.
- Check your spelling.
- Make a neat final copy to publish.

Across the Curriculum

Music: Personal Music Story

For music class, Richard wrote a story about playing in a special family band. The band played zydeco music.

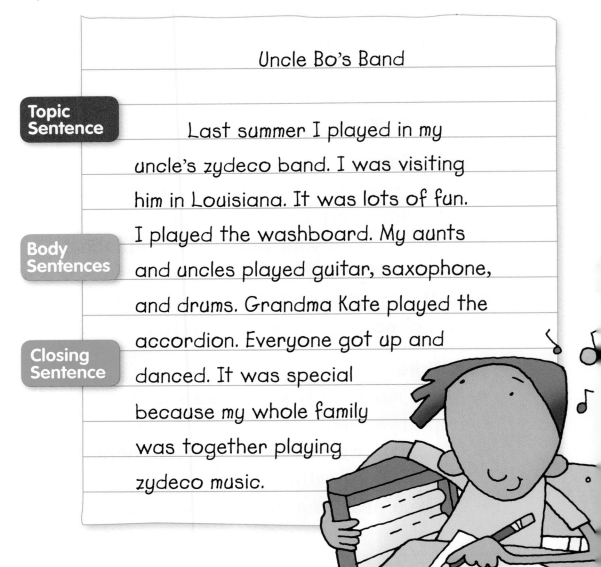

Uncle Bo's Band

Topic Sentence

Last summer I played in my uncle's zydeco band. I was visiting him in Louisiana. It was lots of fun.

Body Sentences

I played the washboard. My aunts and uncles played guitar, saxophone, and drums. Grandma Kate played the accordion. Everyone got up and

Closing Sentence

danced. It was special because *my whole family was together playing zydeco music.*

▶ Writing Tips

Before You Write

- List times when you played an instrument or listened to music.
- Choose one of the times to write about.
- Use a cluster to gather details about the experience.

Cluster

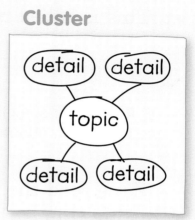

During Your Writing

- In the **topic sentence**, tell what the experience was.
- In the **body** of your paragraph, tell what happened.
- In the **closing sentence**, tell why this experience was special for you.

After You Write

- Read your paragraph. Did you write about just *one* special time?
- Check your capitalization and punctuation.
- Check your spelling.
- Make a neat final copy to publish.

Writing for Assessment

You may be asked to write a paragraph on a test. This is called responding to a **writing prompt**.

Writing Prompt

Remember something you did for the very first time. Write one paragraph about this experience.

Zane read the prompt and thought about interesting things that he'd done for the first time. He made a list of those experiences and told why each was special.

List of Experiences

What was the experience?	Why was it special?
jumped on trampoline	felt like flying
jumped off high board	long fall, big splash
scored a soccer goal	only goal of game

Zane circled the experience he wanted to write about.

Zane's Paragraph

My High Jump

Last summer, Aunt Shandi took me to a pool. It was very hot outside. Kids were splashing and swimming. They were laughing and yelling. I saw the high diving board. It is at the deep end of the pool. I'd never used the high board. Aunt Shandi said I could jump. I climbed up the big ladder. It was scary on the board. The water looked a long way down. I took a deep breath and jumped. Down, down I went. The water made a great big splash around me. I quickly swam to the top. It was great!

Practice

Think about something you did for the first time. Make a list like the one on page **94**. Tell why your experience was special.

Expository Writing

Everyone is good at something. You may be a great soccer player or a star speller. You can teach other people. In this section, you will write directions, a how-to essay, an invitation, and a classroom report.

What's Ahead

- Writing an Expository Paragraph
- Writing an Expository Essay
- Writing Across the Curriculum
- Writing for Assessment

Writing an Expository Paragraph

Max wrote an expository paragraph. **Expository** means *to explain.* Max wrote directions to help a new student find the school lunchroom.

You can write directions, too! You can explain how to get someplace.

Max's Paragraph

How to Find the Lunchroom

Topic Sentence

It is easy to get from our classroom to the lunchroom. First,

Body Sentences

you leave our classroom and turn left. Then go to the trophy case, turn right, and stop. Look straight ahead of you to the end of the hall. What do

Closing Sentence

you see? You've found the lunchroom!

- The **topic sentence** introduces the subject.
- The body sentences give step-by-step directions.
- The closing sentence restates the main idea.

Prewrite ▶ Choose a topic.

Think about places in your school that you could go to from your classroom. Talk with a partner about directions you could write.

1. List three or four places in your school.
2. Circle the one you want to write about.

List of Places

gym
office
(lunchroom)
art room

Prewrite ▶ Gather your details.

1. Draw a simple map that shows the path from your classroom to your destination.
2. Label at least one place you pass.

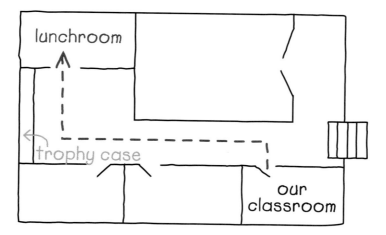

You can use **time order** and **place order** words to make your directions easy to follow. Here are some to choose from.

Time Order Words			Place Order Words		
after	first	before	right	up	ahead
then	next	when	down	left	beside

Writing Create your paragraph.

Remember that each part of your paragraph has a special job.

 **Write** ▶ **Write your first draft.**

1. First, write your **topic sentence**. It tells what your paragraph is about. Write your own sentence or finish the sentence below.

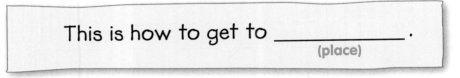

This is how to get to _____.
(place)

2. Next, write your body sentences. Look at your map. Write sentences that tell how to get from your classroom to the other place. Use time and place order words to make your directions clear.

3. Finally, write your own closing sentence about your main idea or finish the sentence below.

You found the _____!
(place)

Revising and Editing

After Max wrote his directions, he changed some parts. Use the checklist below to make your directions better.

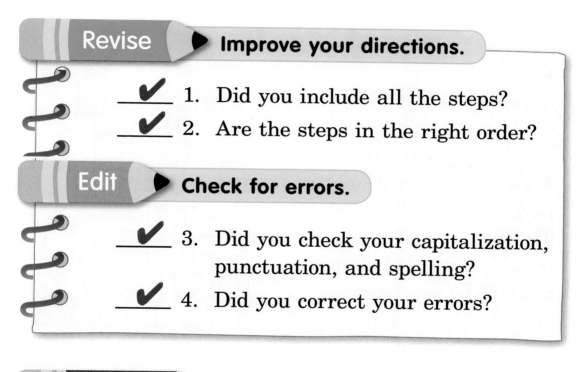

Revise ▶ **Improve your directions.**

✔ 1. Did you include all the steps?

✔ 2. Are the steps in the right order?

Edit ▶ **Check for errors.**

✔ 3. Did you check your capitalization, punctuation, and spelling?

✔ 4. Did you correct your errors?

Publish ▶ **Make a neat final copy.**

1. Print a neat copy of your directions.
2. Add a map if you wish.

Writing an Expository Essay

Emily likes to string beads. Maria knows how to grow flowers, and Jamar makes clay animals. Ty flies kites. Everyone is good at something. What special activity do you enjoy?

In this chapter, you will explain something you can do.

Goals for Writing

The traits below will help you write an expository essay that explains how to do something.

Ideas **Choose a *how-to* topic and explain it.**

Organization **Put the steps in the right order.**

Word Choice **Use words that are interesting and clear.**

Conventions **Check your capitalization, punctuation, and spelling.**

Ty's Expository Essay

How to Fly a Kite

Beginning

You can fly a kite. You will need a kite, a kite tail, lots of string, and a windy day. You should also find a big, open place to fly your kite.

Middle

First, stand with your back to the wind. Next, have a friend hold up the kite. When the wind blows, your friend should let go of the kite. Then run fast and let out some more string. Don't worry if your kite crashes. That happens. Just keep trying.

Ending

Flying a kite is fun. You never know how high or how far your kite will go. Try flying a kite with a friend!

The Parts of an Essay

Ty wrote about how to fly a kite. Look at the parts of his essay.

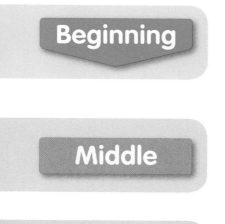

Beginning

The first paragraph **names** the topic. It also tells the reader what supplies are needed.

Middle

The middle paragraph **explains** how to do the activity.

Ending

The last paragraph **tells** why the activity is fun.

After You Read

- **Ideas** (1) What details teach you how to fly a kite?
- **Organization** (2) What time order words did Ty use?
- **Word Choice** (3) Find one sentence that contains clear, interesting words.

Prewriting **Choose a topic.**

Think about fun activities you can do. Maria wrote a list of activities she likes to do.

Maria's List

I can

    make a salad.

    wash my dog.

    (grow a flower.)

    play soccer.

Maria thought about each activity. She decided it would be easy to tell someone how to grow a flower. She circled her choice.

Prewrite ▶ **Choose a topic.**

1. List activities you like to do.
2. Circle the activity that you could explain to a friend. This is your topic.

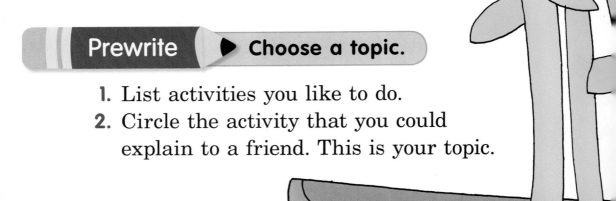

Remember the steps.

Maria thought about what she did to grow a flower. Then she drew simple pictures of the steps. She numbered them and added words about the details.

Maria's Pictures

1	2	3
pot	dirt	seed
4	5	6
sun and water	sprout	flower

Prewrite ▶ **List the steps.**

1. Draw simple pictures of your activity.
2. Number each step.
3. Add words about the details.

Writing **Start your essay.**

The beginning introduces the topic or main idea in a topic sentence. Here are two ways you can begin.

Beginning

Middle

Ending

You can ask a question.

> Do you know how to grow a flower?

You can make a statement.

> Learning how to grow daisies is fun.

Maria completed the sentence starters below. She circled the one she liked best.

> Would you like to grow a flower?
>
> I can teach you how to grow a flower.

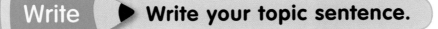

Write ▶ **Write your topic sentence.**

- Create your own topic sentence or use one of the sentence starters above.

Maria's Beginning Paragraph

Maria started her paragraph with her topic sentence. Then she wrote about the supplies. Here is the beginning of her first draft.

> The **beginning** introduces the topic and lists the supplies.

I can teach you how to grow a flower. you need a clay pot, some dirt, and a flower seed. you also need water and sunlight.

Write ▶ Create your beginning paragraph.

1. Start with your topic sentence.
2. Tell what supplies are needed.
3. Use your drawings from your prewriting activity to help you remember the details.

Writing **Write the middle.**

To explain how to do something, you must put the steps in the right order. The **time order** and **place order** words in the chart below can help you connect the steps in your essay.

Beginning

Middle

Ending

Word List

Time Order Words	Place Order Words
first	above
next	below
then	inside
soon	on top of
before long	through
now	near
when	into

Maria's Middle Paragraph

Maria looked at her pictures to remember important details. She used **time order** words and **place order** words to connect the steps in her middle paragraph. (There are some errors because this is Maria's first draft.)

> The **middle** uses details to explain the activity.
>
> Time order and place order words connect the steps.

First, put clean dirt in a clay pot. Next, make a little hole in the dirt. Drop a flower seed into the hole Now put the pot near a sunny window. Give the seed a little water every day. Soon, a tiny, green plant will grow. Make sure it gets sunlight and water. A flower will bloum.

Write ▶ Write your middle paragraph.

1. Look at your prewriting pictures.
2. Then write the steps in the right order.
3. Use time and place order words to connect the steps. (See the red words above.)

Writing **End your essay.**

You can end your how-to essay by telling why the activity is enjoyable. Here are two ways to do that.

Beginning

Middle

Ending

Tell why you enjoy the activity.

Colorful flowers make me happy.

Tell why your reader might enjoy this activity.

Growing flowers can be a great hobby!

Maria's Ending Paragraph

Maria decided to tell why *she* enjoys the activity. She included three reasons in her ending paragraph.

> The ending tells why the activity is enjoyable.

I like growing flowers because they are pretty. It is fun to watch them grow. When they bloum, I pick them for my mom.

Write ▶ **Create your ending paragraph.**

1. Think about why **you** enjoy the activity.
2. Think about why **the reader** might like the activity.
3. Choose one way to end your essay.
4. Include three good reasons in your ending paragraph.

Revising Improve your essay.

After you finish your first draft, it's time to revise. Use the following checklist to make changes.

Revise ▶ Use this checklist.

Ideas

____✔ 1. Did you write about one activity?

____✔ 2. Did you include all the important steps?

Organization

____✔ 3. Did you write a beginning, a middle, and an ending?

____✔ 4. Did you put the steps in the right order?

____✔ 5. Did you use time order and place order words?

Word Choice

____✔ 6. Did you use clear, interesting words?

Maria's Revising

Maria revised her essay. The side notes tell you what changes she made.

I can teach you how to grow a flower. you need a clay pot, some dirt, and a flower seed. you also need water and sunlight.

First, put potting soil ~~clean dirt~~ in a clay pot. Next, make a little hole in the dirt. Drop a flower seed into the hole. Cover it up with dirt. Now put the pot near a sunny window.

Give the seed a little water every day.

Soon, a tiny, green plant will grow.

Make sure it gets sunlight and water. Before long, A flower will bloum.

| Clearer words are added. |

| An important step is added. |

| Time order words are added. |

Editing Check your writing.

After revising, you must check your writing for errors in capitalization, punctuation, and spelling. Use the questions in the checklist below to help you.

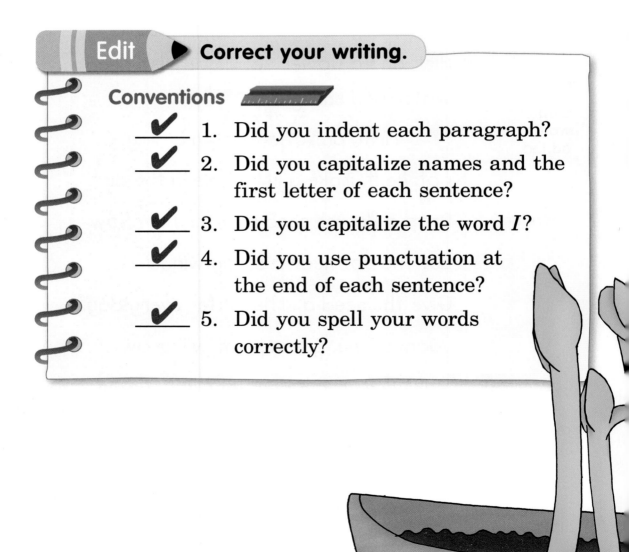

Edit ▶ **Correct your writing.**

Conventions

✔ 1. Did you indent each paragraph?

✔ 2. Did you capitalize names and the first letter of each sentence?

✔ 3. Did you capitalize the word *I*?

✔ 4. Did you use punctuation at the end of each sentence?

✔ 5. Did you spell your words correctly?

Maria's Editing

Two words are capitalized.

A period is added.

A spelling mistake is corrected.

I can teach you how to grow a flower. you need a clay pot, some dirt, and a flower seed. you also need water and sunlight.

First, put potting soil in a clay pot. Next, make a little hole in the dirt. Drop a flower seed into the hole. Cover it up with dirt. Now put the pot near a sunny window. Give the seed a little water every day. Soon, a tiny, green plant will grow. Make sure it gets sunlight and water. Before long,

bloom

a flower will bloum.

Publishing Finish your essay.

How to Grow a Flower

I can teach you how to grow a flower. You need a clay pot, some dirt, and a flower seed. You also need water and sunlight.

First, put potting soil in a clay pot. Next, make a little hole in the dirt. Drop a flower seed into the hole. Cover it up with dirt. Now put the pot near a sunny window. Give the seed a little water every day. Soon, a tiny, green plant will grow. Make sure it gets sunlight and water. Before long, a flower will bloom.

I like growing flowers because they are pretty. It is fun to watch them grow. When they bloom, I pick them for my mom.

Publish ▶ **Make a neat final copy.**

● Draw a picture for your essay if you wish.

Reflect on your writing.

After your how-to essay is finished, take some time to think about your writing.

Thinking About Your Writing

Name: _Maria_

Title: _How to Grow a Flower_

1. The best thing about my essay is

   that I put the steps in the right

   order.

2. The main thing I learned while writing my essay is

   that I have to use clear words to

   explain how to do something.

Using a Rubric

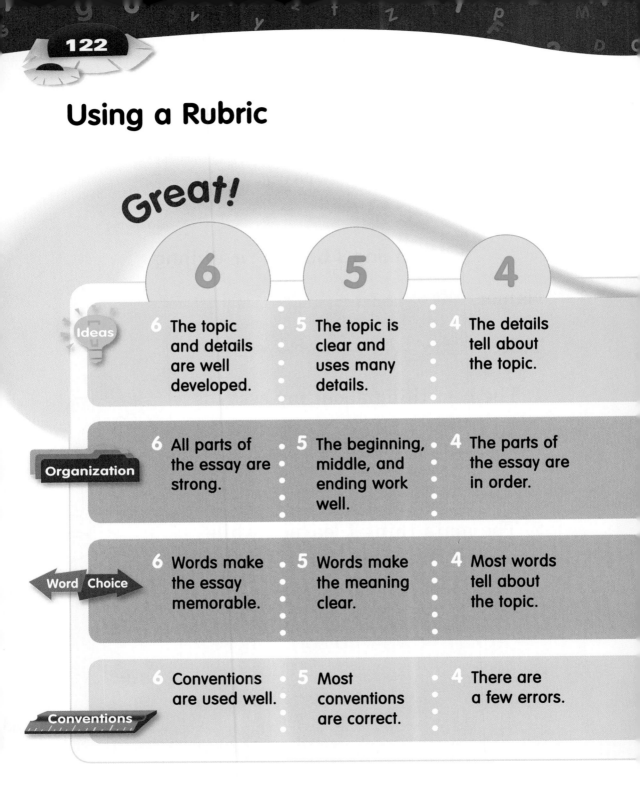

Great!

	6	**5**	**4**
Ideas	6 The topic and details are well developed.	5 The topic is clear and uses many details.	4 The details tell about the topic.
Organization	6 All parts of the essay are strong.	5 The beginning, middle, and ending work well.	4 The parts of the essay are in order.
Word Choice	6 Words make the essay memorable.	5 Words make the meaning clear.	4 Most words tell about the topic.
Conventions	6 Conventions are used well.	5 Most conventions are correct.	4 There are a few errors.

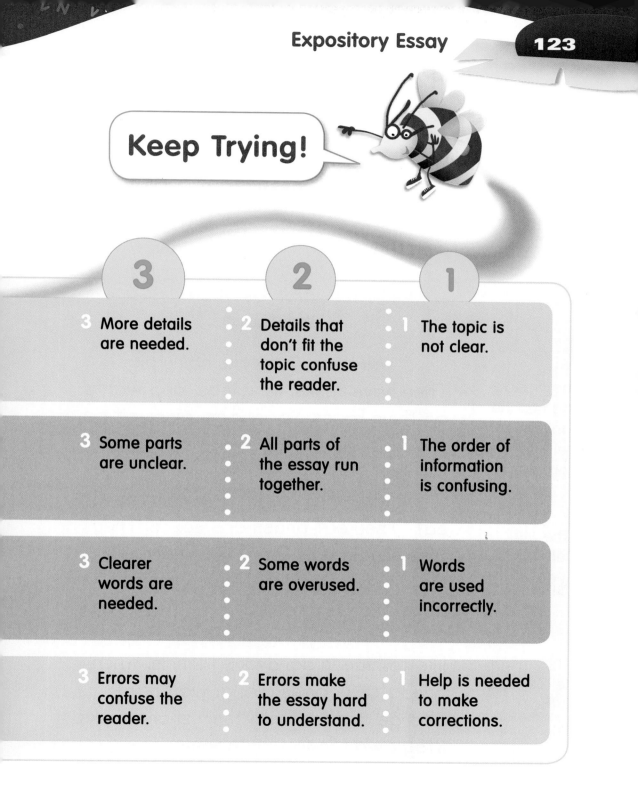

Keep Trying!

3 More details are needed.

2 Details that don't fit the topic confuse the reader.

1 The topic is not clear.

3 Some parts are unclear.

2 All parts of the essay run together.

1 The order of information is confusing.

3 Clearer words are needed.

2 Some words are overused.

1 Words are used incorrectly.

3 Errors may confuse the reader.

2 Errors make the essay hard to understand.

1 Help is needed to make corrections.

Across the Curriculum

Science: An Animal Report

In science class, Kelli wrote an expository essay about an animal. She decided to write her report about warthogs.

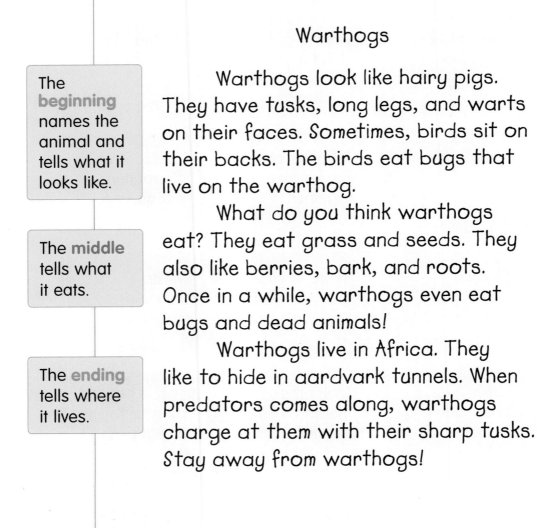

Warthogs

The **beginning** names the animal and tells what it looks like.

Warthogs look like hairy pigs. They have tusks, long legs, and warts on their faces. Sometimes, birds sit on their backs. The birds eat bugs that live on the warthog.

The **middle** tells what it eats.

What do you think warthogs eat? They eat grass and seeds. They also like berries, bark, and roots. Once in a while, warthogs even eat bugs and dead animals!

The **ending** tells where it lives.

Warthogs live in Africa. They like to hide in aardvark tunnels. When predators comes along, warthogs charge at them with their sharp tusks. Stay away from warthogs!

▶ Writing Tips

Before You Write

- Think of an animal.
- Read about the animal.
- Gather details in a chart.

Gathering Chart

Name of topic
_____

1. What does it looks like?

2. What does it eat?

3. Where does it live?

During Your Writing

- In the **beginning** paragraph, name the animal and tell what it looks like.
- In the **middle** paragraph, tell what it eats.
- In the **ending** paragraph, tell where it lives.

After You Write

- Make sure you wrote a beginning, a middle, and an ending paragraph.
- Revise your writing to make it better.
- Check for capitalization, punctuation, and spelling errors.
- Make a neat final copy.

Across the Curriculum

Practical Writing: An Invitation

In class, Paulo wrote an invitation asking his aunt to come to a special event at his school.

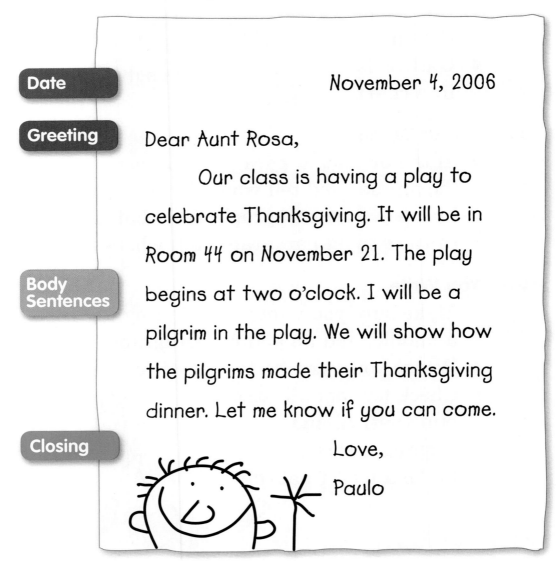

Date

November 4, 2006

Greeting

Dear Aunt Rosa,

Body Sentences

Our class is having a play to celebrate Thanksgiving. It will be in Room 44 on November 21. The play begins at two o'clock. I will be a pilgrim in the play. We will show how the pilgrims made their Thanksgiving dinner. Let me know if you can come.

Closing

Love,

Paulo

▶ **Writing Tips**

Before You Write

- Think of a special event.
- Answer the 5 W's.
    Who will you invite?
    What is the event?
    When will it take place?
    Where will it take place?
    Why should people
    attend the event?

5 W's Chart

Who?	
What?	
When?	
Where?	
Why?	

During Your Writing

- Begin with the **greeting**.
- Answer *what*, *when*, *where*, and *why*.
- Sign your name after the **closing** word.

After You Write

- Make sure you included all the parts of the invitation.
- Check for the answers to the 5 W's.
- Revise your work to make it even better.
- Check your capitalization, punctuation, and spelling.

Writing for Assessment

You may be asked to write an expository paragraph on a test. Yoshi was asked to explain how to play a game.

Writing Prompt

> Think of a game you like to play. Write a paragraph that names it and explains how to play. Tell why you like the game.

Yoshi read the prompt and thought about games he liked to play. He made a list and circled his choice. Then he drew a picture to help him write his paragraph.

Yoshi's Drawing

Ideas List

Games I like to play

water volleyball
the snail
bumper bowling
checkers
baseball

Yoshi's Paragraph

Learn to Play Snail

The **topic sentence** names the game.

The **body sentences** tell how to play the game.

The **closing sentence** gives a final idea about the game.

I know a game called snail. First, you draw a snail on the sidewalk. Make it bigger than your body. Give it an open mouth and a stomach in its middle. You toss a small stone into the snail's mouth. Then you hop on one foot and try to kick the stone into the stomach and back to the mouth. If you do it, you get one point. If you step on a line, you don't get a point. You can play with a friend. Each player takes five turns. The player with the most points wins. I love this game because it is fun to hop.

Practice

Think about a game you could explain. Make an ideas list and circle your choice. You may want to draw a picture to help you write about the game. Include all the steps in order.

Persuasive Writing

Healthy kids are happy kids! That is one child's **opinion**. Your opinion lets others know how you feel about a topic.

In persuasive writing, you try to get the reader to agree with your opinion. Who knows? You may even be able to convince the reader to take action!

What's Ahead

- Writing a Persuasive Paragraph
- Writing a Persuasive Letter
- Across the Curriculum
- Writing for Assessment

Writing a Persuasive Paragraph

Eva saw that her friend, Polly, was falling asleep in class. That's not good, Eva thought. She decided to write a paragraph to persuade her classmates to get more sleep at night.

In this chapter, you will write a persuasive paragraph. You will try to convince your classmates to make healthy choices.

Eva's Paragraph

Go to Sleep!

Topic Sentence   You should get ten hours of sleep each night. Sleep helps you stay healthy and happy. It gives your body **Body Sentences** and brain a rest from working hard at school. Best of all, sleep gives you energy to do fun things, like jumping **Closing Sentence** rope and riding bikes. So every night, you should go to bed and get plenty of sleep!

- The **topic sentence** shares your opinion.

- The body sentences give two or three reasons for your opinion.

- The closing sentence tells the reader what action to take.

Prewriting Choose a topic.

Eva made a cluster to help her find a topic for a persuasive paragraph.

Eva's Cluster

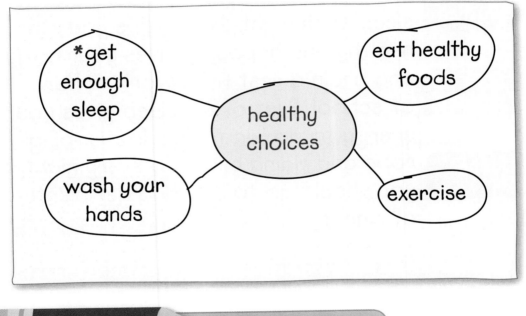

Prewrite ▸ **Choose a topic.**

1. Make a cluster to show ways that students can be healthier.
2. Then put a star by your choice.

Gather details.

Eva wrote an opinion. It explained how she felt about sleep.

You should get ten hours of sleep each night.

Prewrite ▶ **Write your topic sentence.**

1. Write your opinion about one way for students to be healthier.
2. Create your own sentence or finish the sentence below.

You should _____.

Eva listed reasons for her opinion. She circled the most important reason.

Eva's Reasons

Sleep helps you to be healthy and happy.
Sleep lets your body and brain rest.
Sleep gives you more energy.

Prewrite ▶ **List your reasons.**

• Circle your most important reason.

Writing Create your first draft.

Remember that each part of a paragraph has a special job.

- The **topic sentence** tells the opinion.
- The body sentences give reasons for the opinion.

 Write ▶ **Begin your first draft.**

1. Start with your topic sentence. It tells your opinion about **one** way students can be healthier.
2. In the body, write a sentence for each of your reasons. Put the most important reason last.

End with a call to action!

The last sentence of your paragraph is a **call to action**. It persuades the reader to do something. Power words like *you should* or *make sure to* will make your ending strong.

 **Write** ▶ **Write a closing sentence.**

- Ask the reader to take action.

Revising and Editing

After Eva finished her first draft, she used a checklist to improve her paragraph. Use the checklist below to make your paragraph better.

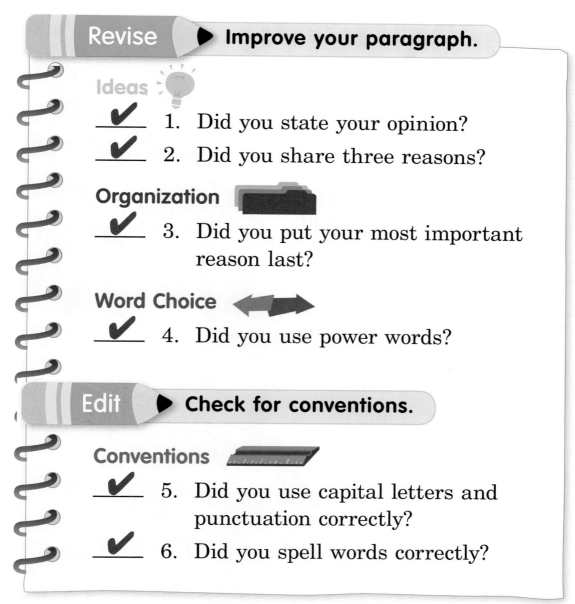

Revise ▶ **Improve your paragraph.**

Ideas

✔ 1. Did you state your opinion?

✔ 2. Did you share three reasons?

Organization

✔ 3. Did you put your most important reason last?

Word Choice

✔ 4. Did you use power words?

Edit ▶ **Check for conventions.**

Conventions

✔ 5. Did you use capital letters and punctuation correctly?

✔ 6. Did you spell words correctly?

Writing a
Persuasive
Letter

"No more junk food!"
That was Mary's opinion.
She wondered if she could
do anything about it.
She decided to write a
persuasive letter.

In this chapter, you
will learn how to write
a letter to persuade.
In your letter, you will
tell about one way to
stay healthy.

Goals for Writing

The traits below will help you to write your letter. Read and talk about these goals.

Ideas — Write an opinion sentence and give reasons that support it.

Organization — Put the parts of your letter in the correct order.

Voice — Use power words like *need*, *would*, and *should* to show your feelings.

Conventions — Use correct capitalization, punctuation, and spelling.

Mary's Letter

Date

January 12, 2006

Greeting

Dear Mom and Dad,

    I should eat healthy snacks at home. At school, I tasted broccoli and soy nuts. I even tried yogurt and celery sticks! Guess what? These healthy snacks taste good!

Body

    Vegetables, fruits, grains, and dairy foods are good for me, too. They can help me think, work, and play better. Best of all, they can keep me healthy.

    I think we all should eat healthy snacks. Please buy some the next time you go to the grocery store.

Closing

Love,
Mary

Signature

Parts of a Letter

A friendly letter has five parts.

Date — The date tells when you wrote the letter.

Greeting — The greeting is a polite way of saying, "Hi."

Body — The body is the main part of the letter.

Closing — The closing is a polite way of saying, "Good-bye."

Signature — The signature is the name at the end of the letter.

After You Read

- **Ideas** (1) What is Mary's opinion? (2) What does she want her parents to do?
- **Organization** (3) Which paragraph includes Mary's reasons?
- **Voice** (4) Was Mary polite in her letter?

Prewriting **Choose a topic.**

Conall made a table diagram to help him list ideas for staying healthy. Then he put a star next to the topic he wanted to write about.

Table Diagram

My Ideas for Staying Healthy		
drink water	eat breakfast	* wash your hands

Write your opinion sentence.

Conall filled in the blank below to write his opinion sentence.

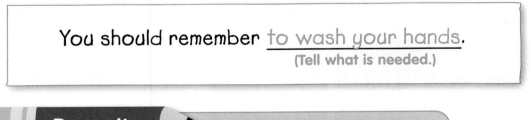

You should remember to wash your hands.
(Tell what is needed.)

Prewrite ▶ **Start your prewriting.**

1. Make a table diagram to list your ideas.
2. Put a star by your choice.
3. Then write your opinion sentence.
   You may use the sentence starter above.

Decide who to write to.

Conall listed groups he could write to. Then he chose one.

List

> my family
> my baseball team
> ✔ Mrs. Martin's class

Gather your reasons.

Conall listed three reasons to support his opinion. He circled his most important reason.

> Topic: Washing your hands
>
> Reasons: keeps your food safe
> keeps you from spreading germs
> keeps you from getting sick

Prewrite ▶ **Finish your prewriting.**

1. Decide who will get your letter.
2. List three reasons to support your opinion.
3. Put a star by your most important reason.

SOAP

Writing Begin your first draft.

The **beginning paragraph** tells your opinion. It shares your idea for staying healthy.

Write ▶ **Write your beginning paragraph.**

1. Start with your opinion sentence.
2. Add details that answer the question *why*.

The **middle paragraph** includes reasons that support your opinion.

Write ▶ **Write your middle paragraph.**

1. Write your reasons.
2. Use power words to persuade the reader.
3. Put your best reason last.

The **ending paragraph** tells what you want the reader to do.

Write ▶ **Write your ending paragraph.**

1. Tell the reader to do something.
2. Be polite.

Conall's First Draft

Here is Conall's first draft. It has a few errors.

Beginning

Give your opinion.

Middle

Include reasons for your opinion.

Ending

Tell the reader to do something.

Dear Mrs. Martin's Class,

Hi. You should remember to wash your hands. Germs live on your skin. they even hide under fingernails!

Wash your hands with soap and warm water. Washing hands keeps germs from spreading to others. It keeps your food safer. Washing your hands can keep you from getting sick.

Make our school a healthyr place. Wash your hands!

Sincerely,

Conall

Revising Improve your letter.

After Conall finished his first draft, he used a checklist to improve his letter. Use the checklist to make your letter better, too.

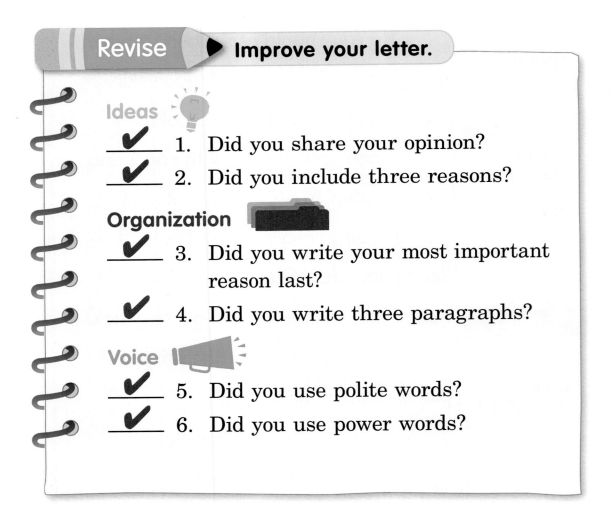

Revise ▶ **Improve your letter.**

Ideas
- ✔ 1. Did you share your opinion?
- ✔ 2. Did you include three reasons?

Organization
- ✔ 3. Did you write your most important reason last?
- ✔ 4. Did you write three paragraphs?

Voice
- ✔ 5. Did you use polite words?
- ✔ 6. Did you use power words?

Conall's Revising

Conall revised his first draft. He cut and added ideas.

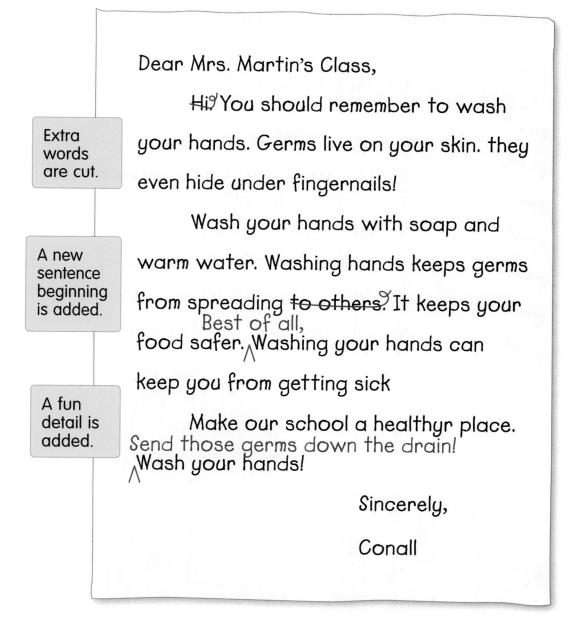

Dear Mrs. Martin's Class,

~~Hi!~~ You should remember to wash your hands. Germs live on your skin. they even hide under fingernails!

Wash your hands with soap and warm water. Washing hands keeps germs from spreading ~~to others.~~ It keeps your food safer. Best of all, Washing your hands can keep you from getting sick

Make our school a healthyr place. Send those germs down the drain! Wash your hands!

Sincerely,

Conall

Extra words are cut.

A new sentence beginning is added.

A fun detail is added.

Edit **Correct your letter.**

Editing means checking and correcting your capitalization, punctuation, and spelling. The following checklist will help you.

Edit ▶ **Check your letter.**

Conventions

✔ 1. Did you begin each sentence with a capital letter?

✔ 2. Did you use a punctuation mark at the end of each sentence?

✔ 3. Did you indent each paragraph?

✔ 4. Did you spell words correctly?

Conall's Editing

Conall made these corrections in his letter.

Dear Mrs. Martin's Class,

You should remember to wash your hands. Germs live on your skin. <u>they</u> even hide under fingernails!

Wash your hands with soap and warm water. Washing hands keeps germs from spreading. It keeps your food safer. Best of all, Washing your hands can keep you from getting sick.

Make our school a healthy place.

Send those germs down the drain! Wash your hands!

Sincerely,

Conall

A capital letter is added.

A letter is corrected.

A period is added.

A spelling error is corrected.

Publish Send your letter.

Before Conall sent his letter, he made a neat final copy. Then he read it again to be sure it was free of mistakes.

Publish ▶ **Make a final copy.**

After making a neat copy of your letter, think about how you will publish it. Sending your letter is one way to publish it. Here are some other publishing ideas:

- Take your letter home and read it to an adult.
- Read it to your class.
- Post your letter on a bulletin board.
- Add it to your writing portfolio.

Conall's Published Letter

January 12, 2006

Dear Mrs. Martin's Class,

    You should remember to wash your hands. Germs live on your skin. They even hide under fingernails!

    Wash your hands with soap and warm water. Washing hands keeps germs from spreading. It keeps your food safer. Best of all, washing your hands can keep you from getting sick.

    Make our school a healthier place. Send those germs down the drain! Wash your hands!

Sincerely,
Conall

Send your letter.

To send your letter, fold it neatly into three parts. Then put it into an envelope.

Remember: The U.S. Postal Service says to use all capital letters and no punctuation when addressing your envelope.

Address your envelope.

1. Write your name and address in the upper left corner.
2. In the middle of the envelope, write the name and address of the person who will get your letter.
3. Put a stamp in the upper right corner.

1 CONALL RIOS
879 64TH AVENUE
MILTON MA 02186

3
Earth Day
USA ¢

2 MRS MARTIN
ROBERT FROST SCHOOL
96 ELM STREET
MILTON MA 02186

Reflect on your writing.

Take a few minutes to think about your writing. Complete the two sentences below.

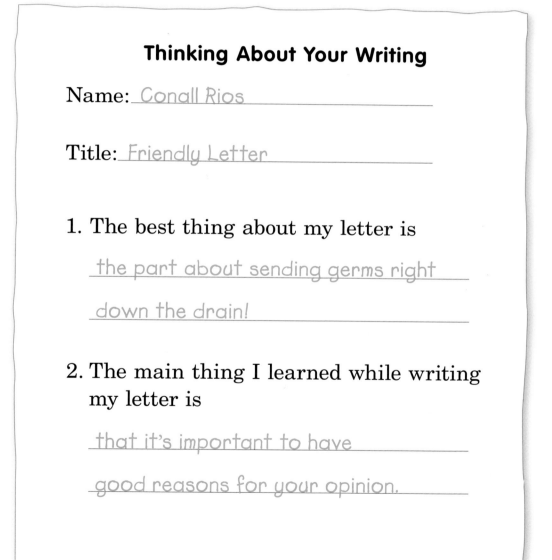

Thinking About Your Writing

Name: _Conall Rios_

Title: _Friendly Letter_

1. The best thing about my letter is

   the part about sending germs right

   down the drain!

2. The main thing I learned while writing my letter is

   that it's important to have

   good reasons for your opinion.

Using a Rubric

Great!

	6	**5**	**4**
Ideas	**6** The opinion and reasons are strong.	**5** Reasons support a strong opinion.	**4** An opinion is given with some reasons.
Organization	**6** All parts of the letter work well.	**5** The letter is written in logical order.	**4** Most of the letter is in order.
Voice	**6** The voice is strong and convincing.	**5** The voice sounds convincing.	**4** In most parts, the voice sounds convincing.
Conventions	**6** Conventions are used well.	**5** Conventions are correct.	**4** There are a few errors.

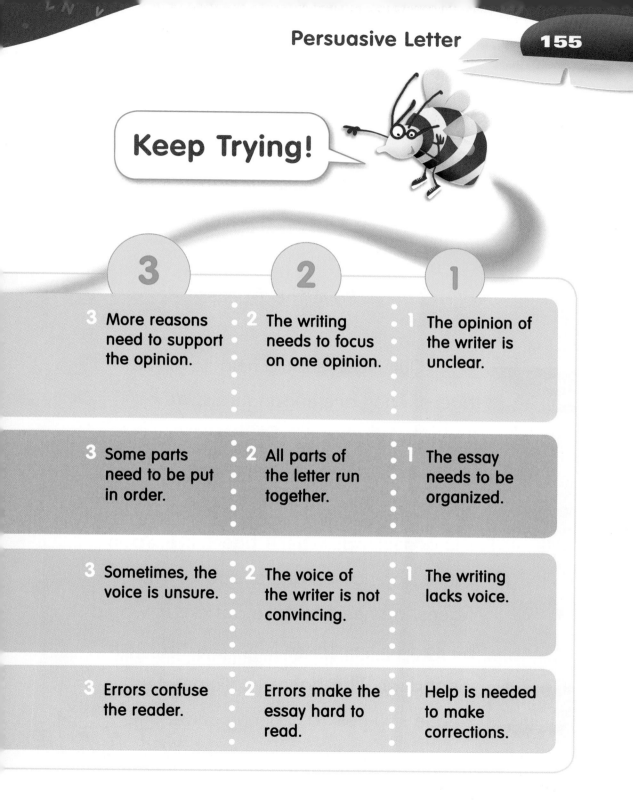

Keep Trying!

3	2	1
3 More reasons need to support the opinion.	**2** The writing needs to focus on one opinion.	**1** The opinion of the writer is unclear.
3 Some parts need to be put in order.	**2** All parts of the letter run together.	**1** The essay needs to be organized.
3 Sometimes, the voice is unsure.	**2** The voice of the writer is not convincing.	**1** The writing lacks voice.
3 Errors confuse the reader.	**2** Errors make the essay hard to read.	**1** Help is needed to make corrections.

Across the Curriculum

Science: Endangered Animal Editorial

For science, Juanita wrote an editorial about an endangered animal for her school newspaper.

Save the Tigers

Topic Sentence

    Our class should help save the tigers. They are endangered. We could have a penny drive and give the pennies to the Wild Tiger Fund. Then people could use the money to save

Body Sentences

the grasslands where tigers live. Soon there may not be any space left for tigers. We need to take action. It would be sad to see these big, beautiful cats disappear. The tigers really need us.

Closing Sentence

Please say yes to a penny drive!

▶ **Writing Tips**

Before You Write

- Think of a cause that you have discussed in class.
  - save endangered animals
  - clean up the environment
- Use a cluster to gather reasons.

Cluster

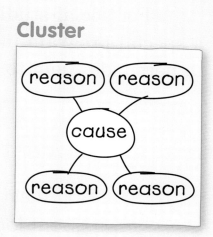

During Your Writing

- In the **topic sentence**, name your cause.
- In the body of your paragraph, give the reasons for supporting this cause.
- In the closing sentence, ask your reader to take action.

After You Write

- Make sure you included important reasons.
- Check capitalization, punctuation, and spelling.
- Make a neat final copy.

Across the Curriculum

Social Studies: Flier for an Event

For social studies, Henry invited his family to a special program in his classroom. He made a flier to persuade them to attend the program.

Meet the Pioneers!

Play their games. Sample their foods. Learn about log cabins. Sing pioneer songs and see a covered wagon.

Who: Mrs. Chua's Class
What: An Evening with the Pioneers
When: 6:30 P.M. on Friday, February 25
Where: Room 20, Bain Elementary School

We will have lots of fun!
PLEASE COME!

▶ Writing Tips

Before You Write

- Think of an event that your class will present.
- Gather details in a 5 W's chart.

5 W's Chart

Who?	
What?	
When?	
Where?	
Why?	

During Your Writing

- Name the event in the title of the flier.
- In a short paragraph, tell what will happen at the event.
- List who, what, when, and where facts.
- Add a sentence to tell why people should attend.

After You Write

- Be sure you included the 5 W's facts.
- Check your capitalization, punctuation, and spelling.
- Make a neat final copy of your flier.

Writing for Assessment

You may be asked to write a persuasive paragraph for a writing assessment. Lila responded to the following writing prompt.

Writing Prompt

> Imagine that your class can take a field trip to any place you have studied. Choose a place. In one paragraph, persuade your class to go there.

Lila read the prompt and thought about places she had studied. She decided to write about going to Washington, D.C. Then she listed reasons why the class should go there.

List of Reasons

1. We could go to the White House.
2. We might meet the president.
3. We could visit the National Zoo.

Lila circled her best reason.

Lila's Paragraph

A Capital Idea

Our class should go to Washington, D.C. It is an exciting city with many things to see and do. First, we'll visit the National Zoo. Next, we could see the White House where many presidents have lived. Best of all, we might even meet the president. We should plan a field trip to Washington, D.C. Let's do it!

Practice

Think about a place you would like to visit on a field trip with your class. Choose one place. Make a list of reasons like the list on page **160**. Then write a call to action.

Responding to Literature

Don't keep a good book to yourself. Tell your friends about it! Talking about books can be fun. Another way to share your ideas is to write about the books you've read.

In this section, you will write about some of your favorite books. You will also learn to compare books and respond to a poem.

What's Ahead

- Writing a Response Paragraph
- Reviewing a Fiction Book
- Reviewing a Nonfiction Book
- Comparing Fiction Books
- Responding to a Poem
- Writing for Assessment

Writing a
Response
Paragraph

After Mark read a story, he wrote about how he was like one of the characters. Look at the three parts of Mark's paragraph.

Mark's Paragraph

By Myself

Topic Sentence

I am like Frog in the book <u>Days with Frog and Toad</u> by Arnold Lobel. In the story, Frog writes Toad a note. It says, "I went out, and I want to be alone." Toad thinks Frog does

Body Sentences

not want to be his friend, but Frog just wants to be by himself so he can think. Sometimes I like to be alone like Frog. Maybe I will write my friends

Closing Sentence

a note like that. I hope they will understand how I feel.

- The **topic sentence** tells what the paragraph is about.

- The body sentences give details about the topic or main idea.

- The closing sentence shows one more idea about the topic.

Prewriting Gather details.

Mark finished some sentence starters to gather details about the book he read. On your own paper, complete these sentences about a book you'd like to write about.

Prewrite ▶ **Finish sentence starters.**

1. The title of this book is _Days with Frog and Toad._

2. The author is _Arnold Lobel._

3. I am like _Frog_ because _sometimes I like to be alone._

4. The part of the story that shows this is _a note Frog writes to Toad. It says that Frog wants to be alone._

Writing Create your first draft.

Use the details from your finished sentences to write your paragraph. Remember to include a topic sentence, body sentences, and a closing sentence.

Write ▶ **Write your paragraph.**

1. Write your **topic sentence**.

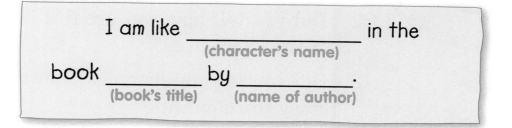

I am like _____ in the
            (character's name)
book _____ by _____.
    (book's title)   (name of author)

2. Write body sentences. Show how you are like the character. Use one example from the story. (See page **166**, number 4.)

3. End with a closing sentence. Share one last idea about your topic.

Revising Improve your paragraph.

Revise your paragraph by changing parts to make it even better.

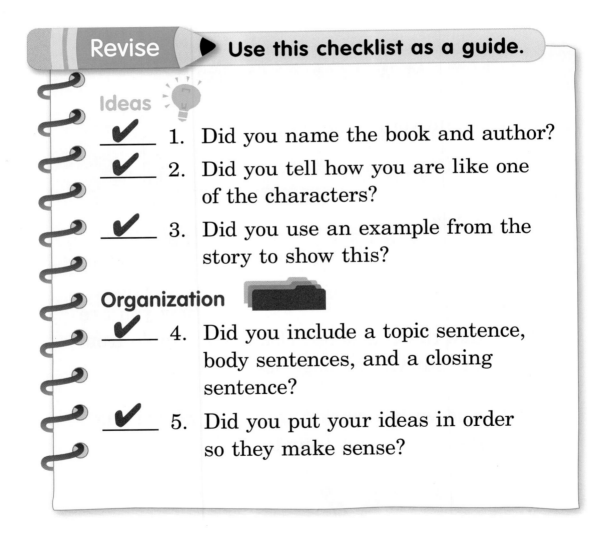

Revise ▶ **Use this checklist as a guide.**

Ideas

✔ 1. Did you name the book and author?

✔ 2. Did you tell how you are like one of the characters?

✔ 3. Did you use an example from the story to show this?

Organization

✔ 4. Did you include a topic sentence, body sentences, and a closing sentence?

✔ 5. Did you put your ideas in order so they make sense?

Editing Check for conventions.

Edit your paragraph by making sure that you followed the rules.

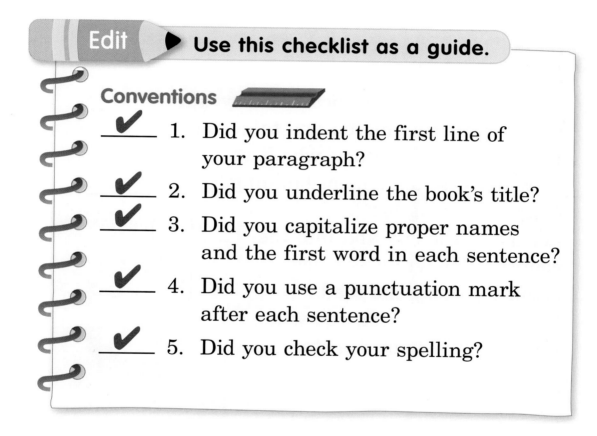

Edit ▶ **Use this checklist as a guide.**

Conventions

✔ 1. Did you indent the first line of your paragraph?

✔ 2. Did you underline the book's title?

✔ 3. Did you capitalize proper names and the first word in each sentence?

✔ 4. Did you use a punctuation mark after each sentence?

✔ 5. Did you check your spelling?

Publish ▶ **Share your work.**

1. Make a neat final copy.
2. Read your paragraph to a classmate.

Reviewing a
Fiction Book

A make-believe (fiction) story can spark your imagination and take you to another world! Stacy, who lives in a high-rise apartment building, enjoyed reading her book. It took her out of the city and into the country. She wrote a review about the story she read.

In this chapter, you will write a review about a story you have read.

Stacy's Book Review

Special Places

All the Places to Love was written by Patricia MacLachlan. In the story, a boy named Eli lives on a farm. He wants to share his special places with his new baby sister.

My favorite part is when Baby Sylvie is born. Eli thinks about showing her the marsh. It is his favorite place. A turtle lives there, and baby ducklings swim in the water.

You should read this book. The words sound like a poem, and the pictures are pretty. If you live in the city, Eli will share his farm with you.

After You Read

- **Ideas** (1) What is the book about?
  (2) Share two things that you learned.

Prewriting Choose a book.

Zola has two favorite books. She made a question grid to help her decide which one to write about. Then she circled her choice.

Zola's Question Grid

What is the title?	Who is the author?	Why do I like the book?
<u>Cloudy with a Chance of Meatballs</u>	Judi Barrett	It is very funny when a big pancake falls on the school.
(<u>Nate the Great, San Francisco Detective</u>)	Marjorie Weinman Sharmat and Mitchell Sharmat	I like mysteries. I enjoyed trying to solve the case.

Prewrite ▶ **Make a question grid.**

1. Write down the titles and authors.
2. Give your reason for liking each story.
3. Circle the title you will write about.

Gather important details.

Zola made a 5 W's chart. It helped her gather details about the book.

Zola's 5 W's Chart

Who?	What?	When?	Where?	Why?
Nate, his dog Sludge, and Duncan were there.	Duncan lost his joke book. Nate helped him find it.	The story happened yesterday.	The story happened in San Francisco.	Duncan made a mess at the Pancake House.

Prewrite ▶ **Make a 5 W's chart.**

1. Read Zola's chart above.
2. Make a 5 W's chart for your book.

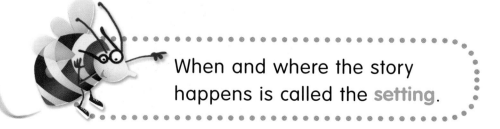

When and where the story happens is called the setting.

Writing Create the beginning.

The first paragraph of your book review names the book and the author. It also tells what the book is about.

Beginning

Middle

Ending

Zola's Beginning Paragraph

Nate the Great, San Francisco Detective was written by Marjorie Weinman Sharmat and Mitchell Sharmat. In this story, Nate goes to San Francisco. He helps a boy named Duncan look for a lost book. Nate is a great detective because he finds lots of clues.

Write ▶ Create your beginning paragraph.

Your beginning paragraph should answer these questions.

- What is the book's title?
- Who is the author?
- What is the book about?

Choose details carefully.

In Zola's beginning paragraph, she did not give away any of the surprises or the story's ending. She used just enough details to make her friends want to read the book for themselves.

Practice

Here is another beginning paragraph about Zola's book. Find two sentences that give away surprises. Tell why these sentences should be left out.

(1) Nate the Great, San Francisco Detective was written by Marjorie Weinman Sharmat and Mitchell Sharmat. (2) The story happens in San Francisco. (3) Nate, the detective, helps a boy named Duncan look for a lost book. (4) It is in the bookstore on the wrong shelf. (5) In the end, the mystery is solved.

Writing **Create the** middle.

The middle paragraph tells about your favorite part of the book. The details are written in the order in which they happen.

Beginning

Middle

Ending

Zola's Middle Paragraph

The details are in order.

The best part is when Nate digs for clues in a messy bag. He finds dirty napkins, cold pancakes, and a small tub of butter. It gets worse. Sticky maple syrup is on everything!

Write ▶ **Create your middle paragraph.**

Tell about your favorite part of the book. Then share some details about it in time order.

Writing Complete your ending.

The ending paragraph tells why you think your friends will enjoy the book.

Beginning

Middle

Ending

Zola's Ending Paragraph

The ending talks to the reader.

Do you wish you were a detective? You can be one when you read <u>Nate the Great, San Francisco Detective</u>. It is fun trying to solve the mystery. See if you can figure it out before Nate does.

Write ▶ **Complete your ending paragraph.**

Thanks for sharing our book.

Revising Improve your review.

Next, Zola revised her review. She used this checklist as a guide.

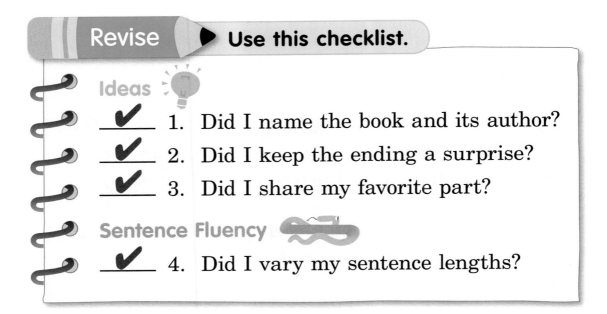

Revise ▶ **Use this checklist.**

Ideas

✔ 1. Did I name the book and its author?

✔ 2. Did I keep the ending a surprise?

✔ 3. Did I share my favorite part?

Sentence Fluency

✔ 4. Did I vary my sentence lengths?

Talk it over.

You can combine short, choppy sentences.

I like to read science fiction ~~books. I also enjoy~~ mysteries. ~~I love~~ and adventure stories, ~~too~~.

I like to read science fiction, mysteries, and adventure stories.

Editing Check your writing.

Then, Zola edited her review. She checked her capitalization, punctuation, and spelling.

Edit ▶ **Use this checklist.**

Conventions

___✔___ 1. Did I capitalize the first word in each sentence and in names?

___✔___ 2. Did I use a punctuation mark after each sentence?

___✔___ 3. Did I underline the book's title?

___✔___ 4. Did I check my spelling?

Zola's Published Review

The Great Nate

Nate the Great, San Francisco Detective was written by Marjorie Weinman Sharmat and Mitchell Sharmat. In this story, Nate goes to San Francisco. He helps a boy named Duncan look for a lost book. Nate is a great detective because he finds lots of clues.

The best part is when Nate digs for clues in a messy bag. He finds dirty napkins, cold pancakes, and a small tub of butter. It gets worse. Sticky maple syrup is on everything!

Do you wish you were a detective? You can be one when you read Nate the Great, San Francisco Detective. It is fun trying to solve the mystery. See if you can figure it out before Nate does.

Publish ▶ **Make a neat final copy.**

Reflect on your writing.

Thinking about your writing can make you a better writer. Think about your book review by finishing the sentences below.

Thinking About Your Writing

Name: Zola

Title: Nate the Great, San Francisco Detective

1. The part of my review I like best is

the ending. I think my question is

interesting.

2. The most important thing I learned is

that it's really important not to give the

whole story away.

Reviewing a Nonfiction Book

Nonfiction books give true information about real people and places. Lee wrote a review about the nonfiction book *Cactus Hotel*. Read his review and learn how to write one, too.

Lee's Book Review

Beginning	A Desert Home
The beginning tells what the book is about.	Cactus Hotel is a book by Brenda Z. Guiberson. It tells about the life of a saguaro cactus. This giant plant grows in the desert.
Middle	
The middle tells three interesting facts.	Here are some interesting facts. When it rains, a saguaro cactus gets fat. A saguaro can live for 200 years. Birds make holes in the cactus. The holes become homes for animals.
Ending	
The ending tells about a favorite part.	My favorite page shows birds, bugs, and rats living inside a saguaro cactus. When one animal moves out, another one moves in. Can you see why it is called a cactus hotel?

After You Read

- Ideas (1) What is the book about?
(2) Share three things that you learned.

Prewriting **Choose a book.**

Debra thought of two nonfiction books. She made a chart to help her decide which one to write about. She starred her choice.

Debra's Chart

Title 1	Jambo Means Hello *
Author	Muriel Feelings
Main Idea	Swahili words tell about life in Africa.
Title 2	How to Dig a Hole to the Other Side of the World
Author	Faith McNulty
Main Idea	You learn what is inside the earth.

Prewrite ▶ **Make a chart.**

1. Write the titles of two nonfiction books.
2. Include the names of the authors.
3. Write the main idea of each book.
4. Put a star (✻) next to the title you will write about.

Gather your details.

Debra wrote several questions. Then she made lists of answers for her book. This helped her collect details for her review.

Debra's Lists

What is the book about?

1. It is about life in Africa.
2. It has a Swahili word for each letter in the alphabet.

What facts do I think are most interesting?

1. School is held outdoors.
2. The Swahili word for children is Watoto.
3. Children take care of cattle and haul water.

Which is *my* favorite part? Why?

My favorite part shows children dancing and playing. It looks like fun!

Prewrite ▶ **Make a list.**

1. Write Debra's questions. Leave room to list the answers.
2. Then answer the questions about your book.

Writing Create your review.

A book review has three parts. It has a **beginning**, a **middle**, and an **ending**. Here is how Debra wrote her review.

1. In the **beginning** paragraph, Debra named the book's title and author. She also told what the book is about.

2. Debra shared at least three interesting facts in the **middle** paragraph.

3. Finally, in the **ending** paragraph, Debra told about her favorite part.

Remember your **beginning**, **middle**, and **ending**.

1.   <u>Jambo Means Hello</u> is a book by Muriel Feelings. It is about life in Africa. The book shows one Swahili word for each letter of the alphabet. Swahili is one of Africa's languages.

2.   Here are some interesting facts. Kids in Africa go to school outside. They have many hard chores to do. They take care of the cattle. They also haul water from the river. The Swahili word for children is Watoto.

3.   My favorite part shows kids dancing and playing. The book says that they sing funny songs and dance with quick steps. I wish I could play with them.

Write ▶ **Complete your first draft.**

Use the information you gathered on pages **184** and **185** to write your review.

Revising Improve your writing.

Debra checked her book review to make sure it answered the five questions below.

Revise ▶ **Use this checklist.**

Ideas

✔ 1. Did you name the book and its author?

✔ 2. Did you tell what the book is about?

✔ 3. Did you share at least three important facts?

✔ 4. Did you tell about your favorite part?

✔ 5. Are your ideas clear?

Editing Check your writing.

Next, Debra edited her review. She checked her capitalization, punctuation, and spelling.

Edit ▶ **Use this checklist.**

Conventions

✔ 1. Did you capitalize the first word in each sentence and in names?

✔ 2. Did you use a punctuation mark after each sentence?

✔ 3. Did you underline the book's title?

✔ 4. Did you check your spelling?

Publishing Finish your review.

Jambo!

Jambo Means Hello is a book by Muriel Feelings. It is about life in Africa. The book shows one Swahili word for each letter of the alphabet. Swahili is one of Africa's languages.

Here are some interesting facts. Kids in Africa go to school outside. They have many hard chores to do. They take care of the cattle. They also haul water from the river. The Swahili word for children is Watoto.

My favorite page shows kids dancing and playing. The book says that they sing funny songs and dance with quick steps. I wish I could play with them.

Publish ▶ **Make a neat final copy.**

Reflect on your writing.

Thinking about your review can help you become a better writer. Complete the sentences below.

Thinking About Your Writing

Name: ___Debra___

Title: ___Jambo!___

1. The part of my review I like best is

___the middle. The facts are interesting.___

_____

_____

2. The most important thing I learned is

___how to tell what the book is about___

___in one or two sentences.___

_____

Comparing Fiction Books

Do you have a favorite book? Travis likes *The Legend of the Indian Paintbrush*. He looked for another book by the author Tomie dePaola. Then he compared the two books. Read his comparison and learn how to write one.

POTATO

Travis's Comparison

Two Long Ago Stories

Beginning

The beginning names the author and the book titles.

My favorite author is Tomie dePaola. I read The Legend of the Indian Paintbrush and Jamie O'Rourke and the Big Potato.

Middle

The middle part compares the two books.

The books are alike because they take place long ago. Both stories are about plants. The books are different, too. In one story, the plant is a potato. In the other, it is an Indian paintbrush. One story takes place in Ireland, and the other happens in America.

Ending

The ending tells why one book is the writer's favorite.

I like Jamie O'Rourke and the Big Potato best because it is funny. I like funny stories.

After You Read

- **Ideas** (1) How are the books alike?
  (2) How are they different?

Prewriting **Select a topic.**

Kamika liked the book *Hedgie's Surprise* by author Jan Brett. For her comparison, she chose another book, *Daisy Comes Home,* by the same author.

Prewrite ▶ **Choose two fiction books by the same author.**

1. Find a book you really like. Write down the author's name.
2. Look in the computer or card catalog at your library to find another book by the author.
3. Read the second book.

Gather details.

Kamika made a Venn diagram to compare the two books she had read. A Venn diagram shows how topics are alike and different.

Kamika's Venn Diagram

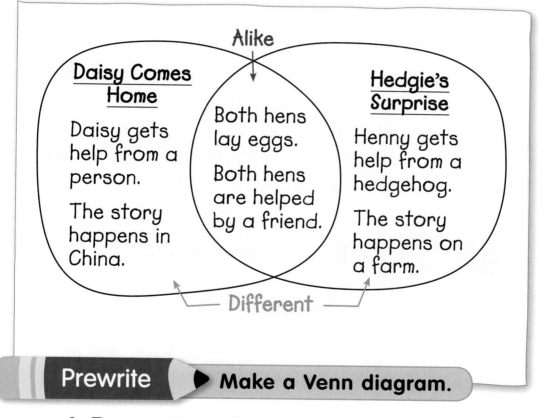

Alike

Daisy Comes Home

Daisy gets help from a person.

The story happens in China.

Both hens lay eggs.

Both hens are helped by a friend.

Hedgie's Surprise

Henny gets help from a hedgehog.

The story happens on a farm.

Different

Prewrite ▶ **Make a Venn diagram.**

1. Draw a Venn diagram to gather details.
2. Write the titles in the outside circles.
3. In the middle, list how the books are alike.
4. In the outside circles, list the differences.

Writing Organize your comparison.

After gathering details, you are ready to write your first draft. Follow the directions below.

Write ▶ Complete your first draft.

1. In the **beginning** paragraph, write the titles and the author's name.
2. In the **middle** paragraph, tell how the books are alike and different. Your Venn diagram will help you.
3. In the **ending** paragraph, tell which book is your favorite and why.

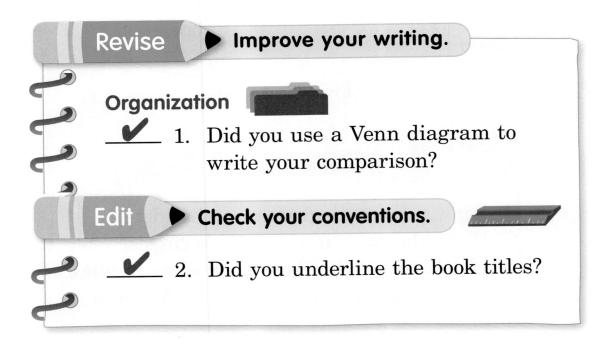

Revise ▶ Improve your writing.

Organization

✔ ____ 1. Did you use a Venn diagram to write your comparison?

Edit ▶ Check your conventions.

✔ ____ 2. Did you underline the book titles?

Kamika's Published Comparison

Two Hens

I read two books by Jan Brett. They are <u>Daisy Comes Home</u> and <u>Hedgie's Surprise</u>.

The books are alike because they are about hens that lay eggs. Both hens get help from a friend. The books are different, too. One hen is named Henny, and she lives on a farm. A hedgehog named Hedgie helps Henny. The other hen is named Daisy. She lives in a sandy yard in China. Daisy's helper is a person named Mei Mei.

I liked <u>Daisy Comes Home</u> best because the setting is China. The pictures show an interesting, faraway place.

Publish ▶ **Make a neat final copy.**

Responding to a
Poem

Snakes

Snakes hiss
like
bacon sizzling,
like
balloons losing air,
like
water on a campfire.

—Eric Williamson

Sean read a poem about snakes.
The poet used **similes** to describe
the sound a snake makes. Similes
compare ideas with the words
like or *as*. In this chapter,
you will respond to a
simile poem.

Sean's Response

Beginning

The beginning tells the title and the main idea.

Middle

The middle shares a favorite simile.

Ending

The ending guesses why the poet wrote this poem.

Sizzling Snakes

"Snakes" is a poem about sounds. It compares the hissing snake to other sounds.

My favorite simile is "Snakes hiss like bacon sizzling." I've heard bacon sizzling on the stove. Ssss! That's what I hear.

I think the poet wrote this poem because he likes snakes. He listens to their hissing sounds and thinks of other things that make the same sound.

After You Read

- **Ideas** (1) How does the writer explain his favorite simile?
- **Sentence Fluency** (2) Does the writer use both long and short sentences?

Prewriting Select a poem.

Read the simile poems on this page. Think about which one you'd like to write about.

Thunder

Thunder rumbles
like
a space shuttle launch,
like
a big bass drum,
like
fireworks!

—Darin Hall

Let's Fly!

Birds fly
like
paper airplanes,
like
leaves in the wind,
like
sparks from a fire.

—Sue Ling

Stars

Stars sparkle
like
Grandfather's eyes,
like
Mother's earrings,
like
my shiny blue shoes.

—Jenna Matson

Leap Frog

Frogs leap
like
funny clowns,
like
kangaroos,
like
tummies on a roller coaster!

—Ty Petski

Prewrite ▶ **Choose your favorite poem.**

Gather details.

Mandy gathered information about a simile poem called "Spring."

Spring

Flower buds wait
like
wrapped presents,
like
chicks inside eggs,
like
pages in a book.

—Ellie Taylor

Sentence Starters

1. The name of the poem is "Spring."

2. The poem is about flower buds.

3. My favorite simile is like pages in a book, because it makes me think.

4. I think the poet wrote the poem because she likes spring.

Prewrite ▶ **Gather details.**

1. Copy Mandy's sentence starters.
2. Write about your poem.

Writing Organize your response.

Follow the plan below to write the response to your poem.

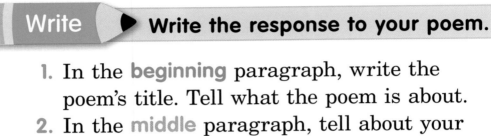

Write ▶ **Write the response to your poem.**

1. In the **beginning** paragraph, write the poem's title. Tell what the poem is about.
2. In the **middle** paragraph, tell about your favorite simile. Explain why you like it.
3. In the **ending** paragraph, tell why you think the poet wrote the poem.

Revise ▶ **Improve your writing.**

Ideas

_____ ✔ 1. Did you tell what the poem is about?

_____ ✔ 2. Did you write about a simile?

Edit ▶ **Check your conventions.**

_____ ✔ 3. Did you put quotation marks around the poem's title?

Mandy's Published Response to a Poem

A Long Wait

"Spring" is a poem about flower buds. The buds are waiting to open. It is the season of spring.

My favorite simile is "Flower buds wait like pages in a book." I thought about that for a long time. Pages in a book are always waiting for somebody to read them. I like similes because they make me think.

Maybe the poet wrote this poem because she is waiting for spring. She might have a flower garden in her backyard.

Publish ▶ **Make a neat final copy.**

- Read your poem and your response to your class.

Writing for Assessment

You may be asked to write about a picture. Terri read the writing prompt below and looked at a picture from a Beatrix Potter story. Then she filled in a 5 W's chart to get plenty of details for her writing.

Writing Prompt

Pretend you are one of the characters in this picture. Write a one-paragraph response.

Tell who you are, what is happening, and how you feel.

5 W's Chart

Who?	Mrs. Hen
What?	talking, peeping, chasing
When?	shopping day
Where?	by the store
Why?	likes to visit

Terri's Response

I am Mrs. Hen, and I am going shopping with **my** chicks. Then I see **my** friend Mrs. Goose. Our babies are peeping loudly. Soon they start chasing each other. It's very noisy, but it's fun visiting on shopping day.

Practice

Look at the picture again. Choose another character. Write your own response.

1. Tell who you are.

2. Describe what you are doing.

3. Explain how you feel.

Creative Writing

"Words are wonderful. By writing them and putting them together, I could make them say whatever I wanted to say. It was a kind of magic." Author Clyde Robert Bulla said these words about creative writing.

In this section, you will use your imagination to write stories, plays, and poems. So, get ready . . . get set . . . imagine!

What's Ahead

- Writing Add-On Stories
- Creating a Play
- Writing Poems

Writing
Add-On Stories

You can stretch your imagination by writing stories. In Angela's **add-on** story, the main character has a problem. One by one, new characters are added to the story. In the end, something surprising happens, and the problem is solved.

Understand the parts of a story.

Every story has four special parts.

Characters

The **characters** are the people or animals in your story.

Setting

The **setting** tells the time and place of your story.

Problem

The **problem** is the trouble the characters face in the story.

Plot

The **plot** is the action in the story.

Practice

1. Read a story.
2. Find its four parts.

Angela's Add-On Story

Go Away, Clouds

Sun had a problem. She was shining, but no one could see her. Clouds were in the way.

Wind tried to help. He huffed and puffed. The clouds wouldn't move.

Then Moon came along. He said, "Go to sleep, Sun. When you wake, the clouds will be gone." So Sun went to sleep, and Moon glowed. Clouds wouldn't move.

Finally, Wolf came along and howled at Moon. "Owoooo!" Suddenly, the clouds got scared and flew away.

In the morning, the clouds were gone. Sun felt happy because everyone could see her now.

After You Read

- Ideas (1) Who is the main character?
  (2) Who are the add-on characters?
  (3) What is the problem?

Prewrite Plan your story.

Hunter's class was writing add-on stories. He answered the 5 W's to make this chart.

5 W's Story Chart

Who is the main character?	Rabbit
What problem happens?	gets stuck
When does it happen?	one morning
Where does the story take place?	outside
Why does it happen?	digs too deep

Prewrite ▶ **Make a 5 W's story chart.**

1. Answer the 5 W's.
2. Then start planning your story.

Prewriting Gather your details.

Hunter used a grid to add new characters and actions to his story. He told how each character helped and what happened next.

Hunter's Story Grid

Character	Action	What happened
Ostrich	used her long neck to reach Rabbit	neck wasn't long enough
Little Kangaroo	jumped into hole to save Rabbit	couldn't jump with Rabbit in her pocket
Python	tied himself to a tree and lowered himself into hole	Rabbit climbed Python like a rope

Prewrite ▶ **Make a grid for your story.**

Writing Begin your story.

Hunter's 5 W's story chart helped him as he wrote his beginning.

Who is the main character?	Rabbit
What problem happens?	gets stuck
When does it happen?	one morning
Where does the story take place?	outside
Why does it happen?	digs too deep

Hunter's Beginning

One morning, Rabbit woke up and began digging. He loved to dig. So he dug and dug a deep hole. When he was done, Rabbit had a problem. He couldn't get out.

Write ▶ Start your story.

- Use your 5 W's story chart to help you.

Writing **Create the middle part.**

Hunter used his story grid to write the middle of his story.

Beginning

Middle

Ending

Hunter's Middle Part

"Help me!" Rabbit cried.

Ostrich heard him and looked into the hole. She stretched her long neck and tried to reach Rabbit. Her neck was not long enough.

Little Kangaroo came along. She hopped into the hole. "Jump into my pocket, and I will jump you out," she said. Rabbit was too heavy. Little Kangaroo jumped out alone.

"Ssssss," someone hissed. It was Python. He said, "I know what to do." He tied himself to a tree to make a long rope. Then Rabbit climbed up Python and out of the hole.

Write ▶ **Create the middle of your story.**

● Use the story grid you made on page **212** to help you.

Writing Make your ending.

In the ending, Hunter told how Rabbit felt when his problem was finally solved.

Beginning

Middle

Ending

Hunter's Ending

Rabbit was excited to be out of the hole. He promised never to dig that deep again.

Write ▶ **End your story.**

- Tell how the main character felt when the problem was solved.

Revising and Editing

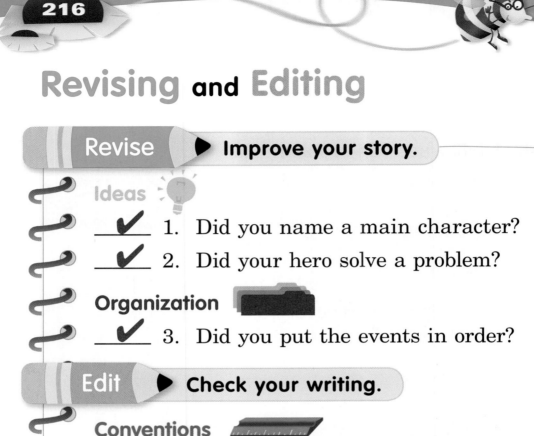

Revise ▶ **Improve your story.**

Ideas

✔ 1. Did you name a main character?

✔ 2. Did your hero solve a problem?

Organization

✔ 3. Did you put the events in order?

Edit ▶ **Check your writing.**

Conventions

✔ 4. Did you follow the rules of writing?

Write ▶ **Add a title.**

Be sure to add a fun title to your story.
Hunter thought of two titles and circled his choice.

The Unlucky Day   (Rabbit's Big Mistake)

Publish ▶ **Make a final copy of your story.**

Hunter's Published Story

Rabbit's Big Mistake

One morning, Rabbit woke up and began digging. He loved to dig. So he dug and dug a deep hole. When he was done, Rabbit had a problem. He couldn't get out.

"Help me!" Rabbit cried.

Ostrich heard him and looked into the hole. She stretched her long neck and tried to reach Rabbit. Her neck was not long enough.

Little Kangaroo came along. She hopped into the hole. "Jump into my pocket, and I will jump you out," she said. Rabbit was too heavy. Little Kangaroo jumped out alone.

"Sssssss," someone hissed. It was Python. He said, "I know what to do." He tied himself to a tree to make a long rope. Then Rabbit climbed up Python and out of the hole.

Rabbit was excited to be out of the hole. He promised never to dig that deep again.

Creating a Play

A play is a story that is acted out. Plays are fun to write because you decide what the characters say and do. You can turn a nursery rhyme into a play. That's what Jade did with this nursery rhyme.

Polly Put the Kettle On

Polly put the kettle on.
Polly put the kettle on.
Polly put the kettle on.
We'll all have tea.
Suki take it off again.
Suki take it off again.
Suki take it off again.
They've all gone away.

Jade's Play

Here is how Jade turned the nursery rhyme *Polly Put the Kettle On* into a play.

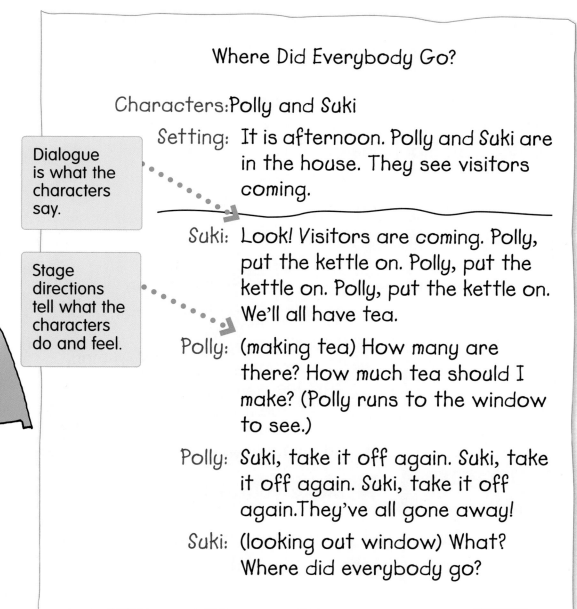

Where Did Everybody Go?

Characters: Polly and Suki

Setting: It is afternoon. Polly and Suki are in the house. They see visitors coming.

Dialogue is what the characters say.

Stage directions tell what the characters do and feel.

Suki: Look! Visitors are coming. Polly, put the kettle on. Polly, put the kettle on. Polly, put the kettle on. We'll all have tea.

Polly: (making tea) How many are there? How much tea should I make? (Polly runs to the window to see.)

Polly: Suki, take it off again. Suki, take it off again. Suki, take it off again. They've all gone away!

Suki: (looking out window) What? Where did everybody go?

Prewriting Choose your rhyme.

Marta's class read nursery rhymes. Marta wanted to make a rhyme into a play. She started planning her play by listing her favorite nursery rhymes.

Marta's List

Baa Baa Black Sheep

Simple Simon

Polly Put the Kettle On

Simple Simon

Simple Simon met a pieman,
Going to the fair;
Says Simple Simon to the pieman,
"Let me taste your ware."
Says the pieman to Simple Simon,
"Show me first your penny." Says
Simple Simon to the pieman,
"Indeed, I have not any."

Prewrite ▶ Make your list.

1. Make a list of your favorite nursery rhymes.
2. Circle the rhyme you will turn into a play.

Name the characters and setting.

Next, Marta listed the characters from the rhyme. Then she wrote about the setting. The setting tells the time and place the story happens.

Marta's T-Chart

Characters	Setting
1. Simple Simon 2. The pieman	Place: At the fair Time: Summer

Prewrite ▶ **Make a T-chart.**

1. List the characters from your rhyme.
2. Then tell about the setting.

Prewriting Put events in order.

Finally, Marta drew pictures. The drawings showed four important events that happened in the nursery rhyme. Marta put them in time order.

Marta's Storyboard

Prewrite ▶ **Make a storyboard.**

1. Draw pictures that show important events from your rhyme.
2. Put your events in time order.

Writing Begin your play.

To begin her play, Marta listed the characters. Then she wrote a few sentences to describe the setting. The setting also tells what will be happening when the play starts.

Beginning

Middle

Ending

Marta's Beginning

Characters:	Simple Simon and a pieman
Setting:	It is summer. The place is the fair. A pieman is selling pies. Simple Simon wants to taste one.

 Write ▶ **Begin your play.**

1. List the characters.
2. Describe the setting.

Writing Create the middle.

The middle tells what the characters say and do. Actions are written in parentheses.

Beginning

Middle

Ending

Marta's Middle

Simple Simon: (shakes hands with the pieman) Good morning, sir. Those are delicious looking pies.

Pieman: Would you like to buy one?

Simple Simon: No. I would like to taste one piece.

Pieman: It will cost a penny for a taste.

Simple Simon: (looks through his pockets and even in his shoes) I don't have a penny.

Pieman: Not one penny? Then no pie for you.

Simple Simon: Not even a taste of pie?

Pieman: No penny. No taste. No pie!

Write ▶ **Complete the middle of your play.**

- Remember to put actions in parentheses.

Writing Create your ending.

Marta ended her play with the main character saying one last important thing.

Beginning

Middle

Ending

Marta's Ending

Simple Simon: (walking off stage, calling to other people at the fair) Does anyone have a penny so I can try some pie?

Write ▶ **Complete your play.**

Add a Title

Marta used her imagination to think of two titles for her play. She circled her choice.

(Just One Tiny Taste)   Simon and the Pieman

Revising and Editing

Revise ▶ **Use this checklist.**

Ideas

✔ 1. Did you list the characters and the setting?

Organization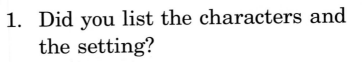

✔ 2. Did you write each character's words next to the character's name?

✔ 3. Did you write events from the nursery rhyme in the right order?

Edit ▶ **Check your writing.**

Conventions

✔ 4. Did you start each sentence with a capital letter?

✔ 5. Did you punctuate your sentences?

✔ 6. Did you check your spelling?

Publish ▶ **Think of a fun title for your play.**

Marta's Published Play

Just One Tiny Taste

Characters: Simple Simon and a pieman

Setting: It is summer. The place is the fair. A pieman is selling pies. Simple Simon wants to taste one.

Simple Simon: (shakes hands with the pieman) Good morning, sir. Those are delicious looking pies.

Pieman: Would you like to buy one?

Simple Simon: No. I would like to taste one piece.

Pieman: It will cost a penny for a taste.

Simple Simon: (looks through his pockets and even looks in his shoes) I don't have a penny.

Pieman: Not one penny? Then no pie for you.

Simple Simon: Not even a taste of pie?

Pieman: No penny. No taste. No pie!

Simple Simon: (walking off stage, calling to other people at the fair) Does anyone have a penny so I can try some pie?

Writing Poems

Alec has fun writing poems. He makes pictures with words as he writes rhyming poems, tongue twisters, and name poems. You can write poems, too. This chapter will show you how.

Alec's Rhyming Poem

Riding

My bike is more fun than TV or a slide.

The tires go bump wherever I ride.

Ants dash away when I rush by

Riding my bike on the Fourth of July.

After You Read

- **Ideas** (1) What does the poem make you see and feel?
- **Organization** (2) Which lines of the poem rhyme?
- **Word Choice** (3) Which word pictures do you like best?

Prewriting **Select a topic.**

Shayna drew pictures of things she likes to do. Then she chose one activity for her rhyming poem.

Shayna's Activities

I will write *my poem about* dancing.

Prewrite ▶ **Draw some pictures.**

1. Draw pictures of activities you enjoy.
2. Choose one activity to write about. Copy the following sentence and fill in the blank.

I will write *my poem about* _____ .
(your activity)

Gather your details.

Shayna imagined herself dancing. Next, she made a sensory chart. She wrote one sentence about dancing for each sensory word.

Shayna's Sensory Chart

Topic: Dancing

See	I see the world spin when I twirl.
Hear	I hear music with a Latin beat.
Smell	I smell fresh air when I dance outside.
Feel	I feel the wind when I dance.

Prewrite ▶ **Make a sensory chart.**

1. Create a chart like the one above for your own topic.
2. Fill in sentences for each sensory word.

Prewriting **Organize your poem.**

Shayna chose interesting words from her sensory chart. She wrote them across the top of her paper. Then she made lists of words that rhyme.

Shayna's Rhyming Lists

dance	twirl	beat	spin
prance	girl	neat	win
chance	whirl	treat	chin
France	swirl	feet	grin
		meet	tin

Prewrite ▶ **Make lists of rhyming words.**

1. Choose some words from your sensory chart that you can rhyme.
2. Use a rhyming dictionary if you can't think of rhyming words.

Writing **Create your poem.**

Now it's time to write your poem. It should have four lines. Use rhyming words at the ends of the first and second lines. Use two more rhyming words at the ends of the third and fourth lines.

Sample Rhyming Lines

I like to make pictures with paper and glue.
I use pretty colors, like purple and blue.

Write ▶ **Complete your rhyming poem.**

1. Look over your chart and rhyming lists.

2. Pick a pair of rhyming words. Write two sentences. Use one rhyming word at the end of each sentence. Pick another pair of rhyming words and do the same thing.

3. Put your sentences together to make a poem.

Revising and Editing

Revise ▶ Use this checklist.

Ideas

✔ 1. Did you choose one activity as a topic?

✔ 2. Did you use ideas from your chart?

Organization

✔ 3. Did you write four lines?

✔ 4. Did you make the first and second and the third and fourth lines rhyme?

Word Choice

✔ 5. Did you use sensory words?

✔ 6. Do your ending words rhyme?

Edit ▶ Check your writing.

Conventions

✔ 7. Did you check your writing for mistakes in capitalization and punctuation?

✔ 8. Did you check your spelling?

Shayna's Published Poem

Shayna Dancing

I love dancing to a Latin beat.

I clap my hands and stomp my feet.

I feel the wind as I spin and twirl.

Look! I'm a happy dancing girl!

Publish ▶ **Make a neat final copy.**

1. Add a title and make a neat copy of your poem.
2. Read your poem to family and friends.

Name Poems

Abigail wrote this name poem. Notice how the letters in her name begin each line. All the words describe Abigail.

An animal lover
Bashful
Interesting
Good
Always on time
Important
Loved

After You Read

- **Ideas** (1) What is the topic of Abigail's name poem?
- **Organization** (2) How is the name poem arranged?
- **Word Choice** (3) What words describe Abigail's personality?

Prewriting **Plan your poem.**

Sean planned his name poem. He listed describing words for each letter in his name.

Sean's Describing Words

S	E	A	N
smart	edits	amusing	nice
scientist someday	excited	actor	nickname is Champ
speaks Spanish	empties the trash	age 8	never naughty
smiles	explores the beach	an amigo	nutritious eater
special			

Prewrite ▶ **List describing words.**

1. Write your name across a piece of paper.
2. List describing words for each letter.

Writing Create your poem.

Write ▶ **Complete your name poem.**

Use your describing words to write your name poem. Remember to do these things when you write.
- Capitalize the first letter of each line.
- Use one or more words on a line.
- Do not use end punctuation marks.

Sean's Name Poem

Speaks Spanish
Explores the beach
Amigo to everyone
Nickname is Champ

Other Kinds of Poems

Try writing these other kinds of poems, too.

ABC Poem

An **ABC poem** uses part of the alphabet to make a list poem.

> Amazing
> Bubbles
> Can
> Dance
> Everywhere.

Tongue Twister

A **tongue twister** is a short, silly story poem. Most of the words begin with the same sound. This is called **alliteration**.

> Wet weather brings wonderful worms who wiggle wildly. Wow!

Shape Poem

A **shape poem** uses the words of the poem to make the shape of the poem's main idea.

Terse Verse

Terse verse is short and funny. It has two rhyming words that have the same number of syllables. The title is the subject.

Joke Book

Smile
File

Lemonade

Pink
Drink

Huge Hog

Big
Pig

Diamond Poem

A **diamond poem** follows a syllable pattern. (Lines two and six name the subject.)

1.	bats	(one syllable)
2.	baseball	(two syllables)
3.	pitch hit run	(three syllables)
4.	bases loaded	(four syllables)
5.	first home run	(three syllables)
6.	baseball	(two syllables)
7.	cheers	(one syllable)

5 W's Poem

A **5 W's poem** is five lines long. Each line answers one of the 5 W's (*Who? What? When? Where?* and *Why?*).

My dog *(Who?)*

curls up *(What?)*

on my bed *(Where?)*

every night *(When?)*

because I let him. *(Why?)*

Report Writing

What do you do when you have a question? Of course, you can ask your teachers and parents. You could also go to the library to find answers to your questions. In this section, you will learn how to find information, write a report, and create a multimedia presentation.

What's Ahead

- Finding Information
- Writing a Report
- Creating a Multimedia Presentation

Finding Information

Ezra and his class were getting ready to write reports. Each student would choose a bird to write about. Their teacher took them to the library to find information. Here's what they learned.

The Librarian

The librarian is a special source of information.

What does a librarian do?

A librarian

- chooses and organizes the library's books.
- recommends books and stories you might like.
- helps you find information.
- knows where everything is in the library.
- helps you with computer searches.

Sources of Information

Libraries may look different from one another, but they have the same types of information. On this page and the next, you will find an example of a library map.

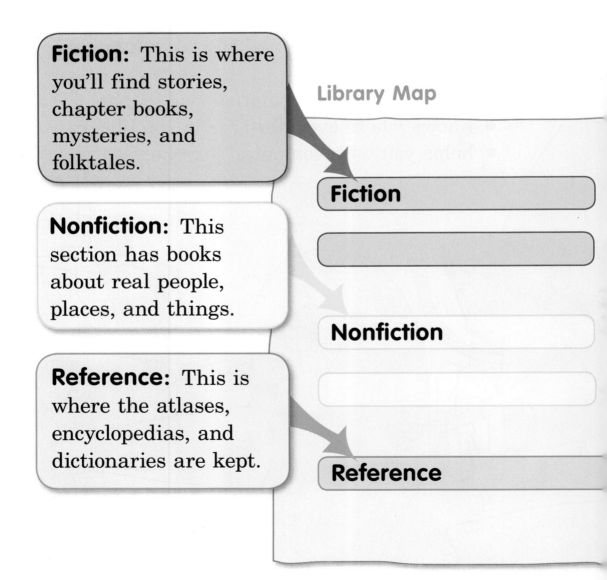

Fiction: This is where you'll find stories, chapter books, mysteries, and folktales.

Nonfiction: This section has books about real people, places, and things.

Reference: This is where the atlases, encyclopedias, and dictionaries are kept.

Library Map

Fiction

Nonfiction

Reference

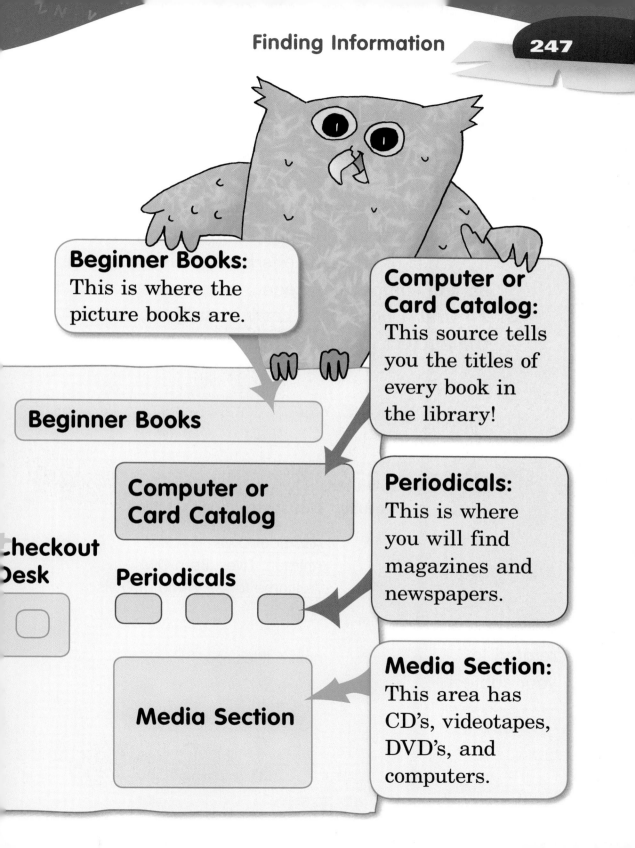

Beginner Books:
This is where the picture books are.

Computer or Card Catalog:
This source tells you the titles of every book in the library!

Beginner Books

Computer or Card Catalog

Checkout Desk

Periodicals

Periodicals:
This is where you will find magazines and newspapers.

Media Section

Media Section:
This area has CD's, videotapes, DVD's, and computers.

The Computer Catalog

A computer catalog gives you three ways to look up a book.

1. If you know the **title** of a book, enter it.
2. If you know the name of the **author**, enter it. A list of the author's books will come up on the computer screen.
3. To find a book on a certain **subject**, enter the subject or a keyword.

A **keyword** is a word or phrase related to your subject.

Keyword: Owl

Results: *Owl* search found 23 titles

All About Owls
Animals' Lives: Barn Owl
Welcome to the World of Owls
Owls

next 4 titles >>>

The Card Catalog

Some libraries keep the information about their books on cards. Every book has a **title**, an **author**, and a **subject** card. They are filed in ABC order.

Title Card

E
598.9
ARN

All About Owls

Arnosky, Jim
All About Owls
Scholastic, 1995

Author Card

E
598.9
ARN

Arnosky, Jim

Arnosky, Jim
All About Owls
Scholastic, 1995

Subject Card

E
598.9
ARN

OWLS

Arnosky, Jim
All About Owls
Scholastic, 1995

An enticing book for young naturalists. Many questions are answered about owls. The watercolor illustrations add to the interest.

Call Numbers

To find a nonfiction book, carefully write down the **call number** from the catalog. Then an adult can help you find the book. The picture below shows how to find *All About Owls* on the bookshelf.

All About Owls   E 598.9 ARN

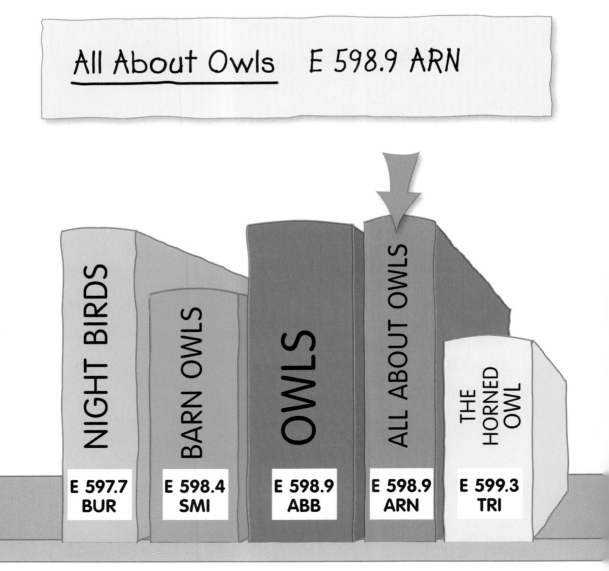

NIGHT BIRDS
E 597.7
BUR

BARN OWLS
E 598.4
SMI

OWLS
E 598.9
ABB

ALL ABOUT OWLS
E 598.9
ARN

THE HORNED OWL
E 599.3
TRI

Parts of a Book

Every book has different parts. Each part either gives information or helps you find information in the book.

Front of the Book

- The **title page** lists the book's title and author. It may also list the illustrator.
- The **table of contents** lists the chapters and their page numbers.

Back of the Book

- A **glossary** lists special words used in the book and gives their meanings.
- The **index** lists topics from the book in ABC order and gives you their page numbers.

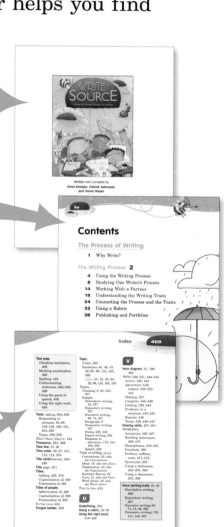

Encyclopedias

Encyclopedias are books that contain articles on many topics. They are arranged in ABC order. To find information about owls, look in the O book.

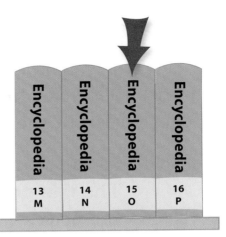

Electronic Encyclopedia

Encyclopedias are also found on CD's or on the Internet. Ask your teacher or the librarian to help you use this type of encyclopedia.

http //www.cooperschool.edu/encyclopedia

Bookmarks

The Cooper School Encyclopedia

Keyword: owls

Related: birds, wild animals, animals of North America

Owls live in many climates. They are birds of prey that hunt other animals. Owls have large eyes, but their ears help them to find their prey at night.

Thesaurus

If you wanted to find another word for *turn*, you could look in a thesaurus. Different words that mean the same thing are called **synonyms**. A thesaurus lists words in ABC order.

Owls turn their heads to search for food.

Thesaurus entry

> **turn**   verb 1. The hands on the clock turn.
> *circle, spin, swivel*

If you like the synonym *swivel*, you could use it instead.

Owls swivel their heads to search for food.

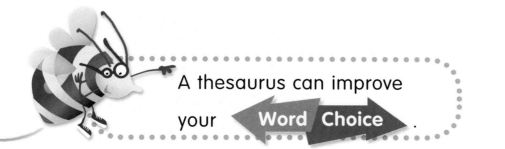

A thesaurus can improve your **Word Choice** .

Dictionary

Dictionaries are found in the reference section. A dictionary tells you many things about words.

Guide Words

These words are found at the top of each page. They show the first and last entry words.

Entry Words

These are the words listed in ABC order on each page.

Spelling

Each entry word is spelled correctly.

Meaning

The meaning or meanings of each entry word are given.

Example Sentence

Each entry word is used in a sentence.

Some dictionaries show the pronunciation of a word.

ca • nar • y (kə **nâr´** ē)

Sample Dictionary Page

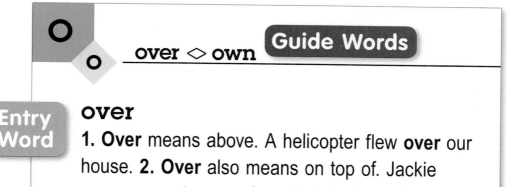

over ◇ own   **Guide Words**

Entry Word

over
1. **Over** means above. A helicopter flew **over** our house. 2. **Over** also means on top of. Jackie wore a sweater **over** her shirt. 3. **Over** also means more than. Lily's father is **over** six feet tall. 4. **Over** can also mean down. Paula knocked **over** a glass of milk.

Spelling

owl
An **owl** is a kind of bird. It has a large head and large round eyes that look straight ahead.
Meaning
Owls come out to hunt at night.

own
Example Sentence
To **own** means to have and keep something.
Jane **owns** a lot of books and toys.

Internet

Another source of information is the Web. For example, the Web sites of zoos and rescue centers would probably have interesting details about owls.

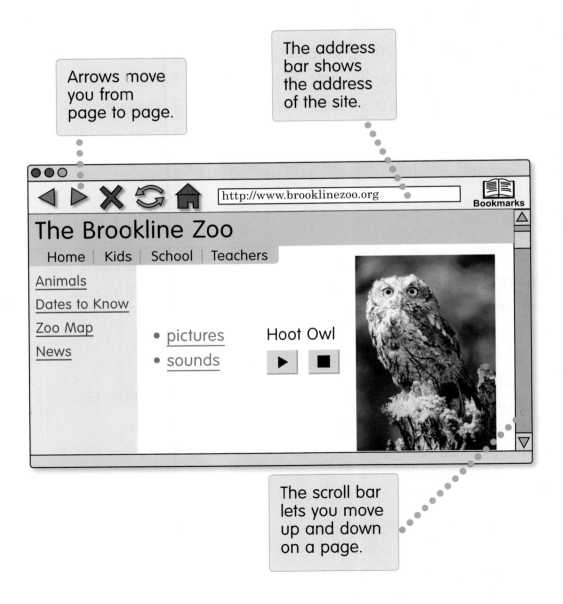

Arrows move you from page to page.

The address bar shows the address of the site.

The scroll bar lets you move up and down on a page.

Periodicals

Magazines and newspapers are also good sources of up-to-date information. They are printed more often than books are. See the sample magazine pages below.

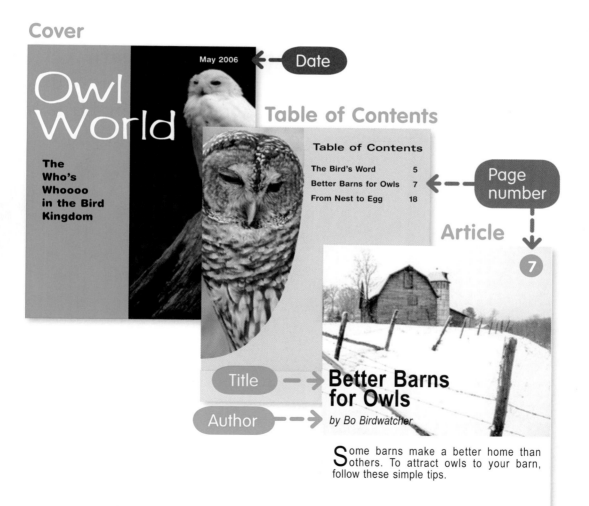

Cover

May 2006 ← Date

Owl World

The Who's Whoooo in the Bird Kingdom

Table of Contents

Table of Contents

The Bird's Word   5

Better Barns for Owls   7 ← Page number

From Nest to Egg   18

Article

7

Title → **Better Barns for Owls**

Author → *by Bo Birdwatcher*

Some barns make a better home than others. To attract owls to your barn, follow these simple tips.

Writing a Report

In a report, you can share what you learn about an interesting topic. In this chapter, you will see how Tori wrote her report about hummingbirds. You can write a report, too. This chapter will show you how.

Tori's Report

Humming Wonders

A hummingbird is an amazing bird. When it flies, its wings go so fast that they hum. That is how it got its name. A hummingbird can fly up, down, forward, and even backward.

The hummingbird is tiny. It is about 3 1/2 inches long. Its feathers are mostly brown and gray, but some are a shiny green, purple, red, or orange.

When a hummingbird eats, it flies like a helicopter. The long beak of the hummingbird pokes into flowers and drinks nectar. A hummingbird likes orange and red flowers. It also eats tree sap and insects. It lives close to the water in forests and gardens.

A hummingbird has an interesting life cycle. The mother bird builds a small nest out of tiny sticks and spiderwebs. She fills the nest with dandelion fluff and cattail fuzz. Then she lays two white eggs. The eggs are the size of peas.

When the chicks hatch, they are very tiny. The mother gathers insects, sap, and nectar to feed her babies. They grow quickly.

A hummingbird seems very smart. The spiderwebs let the nest stretch as the babies grow! I like the hummingbird because it is shiny, beautiful, and just plain amazing.

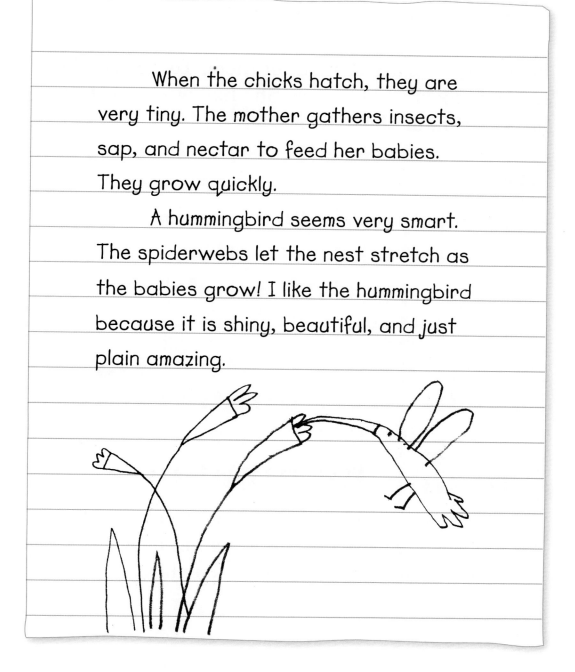

Prewriting Choose a topic.

Tori's teacher wrote the names of birds on the board as the class thought of them. Tori chose the hummingbird as her topic. She had watched them at her grandmother's house.

Topic Ideas

bluebird	hawk	heron	jay
flamingo	ostrich	owl	kiwi
parrot	pigeon	cardinal	tern
penguin	bobwhite	loon	eagle
hummingbird	duck	pelican	dove

Prewrite ▶ **Choose your topic.**

1. Pick a bird you'd like to write about. (If you wish, choose one from the list above.)
2. Find information about your bird.

List your resources.

Tori's teacher and her librarian helped her find many sources of information. Tori listed them.

Tori's Resource List

Books
Hummingbirds by Diane Swanson
Birds by Claude Delafosse

Magazine
Birdwatcher's Digest

Internet
www.hummingbirds.net

Titles of books and magazines are always underlined.

Prewrite ▶ **Look for sources about your bird.**

- Write your own resource list like the one above.

Take notes.

As Tori read her information, she found many facts. She folded a large sheet of paper into eight squares and wrote a heading in each. Then she listed the facts under each heading.

Tori's Gathering Grid

The Body

- long pointy beaks
- shiny green, purple, red, orange, brown, and gray feathers
- wings go so fast
- 3 1/2 inches long

The Food

- nectar from red and orange flowers
- tree sap and insects
- fly and eat at the same time

The Nest

- built by mother bird
- filled with cattail fuzz and dandelion fluff
- tiny sticks and spiderwebs

The Egg

- white
- lays two eggs
- size of a pea

Prewrite ▶ **Make your gathering grid.**

1. To start, fold your paper and write the headings from the example grid.
2. Read your sources and look for facts.
3. Then write the facts under the correct heading.

Where It Lives	Some Amazing Facts
• in mountains, forests, gardens • near water	• the nest can stretch • fly up, down, backward, and forward very fast • wings hum when they fly
The Babies	I like this bird because
• born with no feathers • fly in 2 or 3 weeks	• beautiful, tiny birds • fun to watch

Interview an expert.

Other people may know about your topic. Tori decided to interview her grandmother, who loves to watch hummingbirds.

▶ **Writing Tips**

Before the Interview

- Think of a person who knows about your topic.
- With a parent's help, set up a time and place to interview this person.
- Write questions you would like to ask.
- Take your pencil, notebook, and list of questions with you.

During the Interview

- Ask questions and listen carefully.
- Write the answers on your paper.
- Ask the person to repeat anything you don't understand.

After the Interview

- Thank the person for talking with you.
- Read over your notes.

Sample Interview

1. What do hummingbirds eat?

    sap and insects

    drink nectar with a long tongue

2. Where have you seen hummingbirds?

    at the feeder on the porch

    by the lake on orange lilies

3. Why do you like hummingbirds?

    beautiful, tiny birds

    colored like shiny, bright jewels

4. What is your favorite thing about the
    hummingbird?

    fun to watch

Writing Create your topic sentence.

Start your first paragraph with a topic sentence. It should tell what your report is about. Here are three ways to write your topic sentence.

Beginning

Middle

Ending

> A(n) _____ is an amazing bird.
> (name of bird)
>
> I like the _____ because _____.
> (name of bird)   (why you like it)
>
> Do you know about the _____?
> (name of bird)

Write ► Create your topic sentence.

- Write a topic sentence. You can write your own or use an idea listed above.

Tori's Beginning Paragraph

After Tori wrote a topic sentence, she used two amazing facts from her grid to finish her first paragraph. Tori focused on her ideas and didn't worry about making a few mistakes.

Some Amazing Facts

- the nest can stretch
- fly up, down, backward, and forward very fast
- wings hum when they fly

Tori's Beginning

A hummingbird is an amazing bird. Its wings go so fast that they hum. That is how it got its name. A Hummingbird can fly up down forward and even backward.

Write　▶ **Finish your first paragraph.**

- Use some amazing facts from your grid to write your first paragraph.

Writing Create your middle paragraphs.

Tori used more facts from her grid to write her middle paragraphs. She wrote about the body of the hummingbird in her first middle paragraph.

Beginning

Middle

Ending

Grid

The Body

- long pointy beaks
- shiny green, purple, red, orange, brown, and gray feathers
- wings go so fast
- 3 1/2 inches long

Tori's First Middle Paragraph

> The hummingbird is tiny. It is about
>
> 3 1/2 inches long. Its feathers are mostly
>
> brown and gray, but some are a shiny
>
> green, purple, red, or orange.

Write ▶ **Create the middle of your report.**

- Write your middle paragraphs. Use ideas from your grid. Group them into four main ideas as shown below.

1. Describe the bird's body.
2. Tell about its food and where it lives.
3. Tell about its nest and eggs.
4. Tell about the babies.

Writing **Complete your** ending.

Tori shared another amazing fact in her last paragraph. Then she told why she liked the bird.

Beginning

Middle

Ending

Grid

Some Amazing Facts

- the nest can stretch
- fly up, down, backward, and forward very fast
- wings hum when they fly

I like this bird because

- beautiful, tiny birds
- fun to watch

Tori's Ending Paragraph

A hummingbird seems very smart. The spiderwebs let the nest stretch as the babies grow! I like the hummingbird because it is shiny, beautiful, and just plain amazing.

Write ▶ **End your report.**

1. Share one more amazing fact from your grid.
2. Tell why you really like the bird.

Revising Improve your report.

When you revise, the traits can help you make changes to parts of your report.

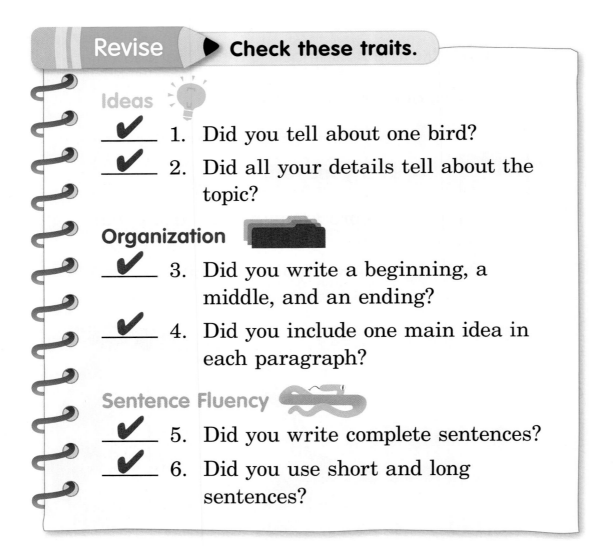

Revise ▶ **Check these traits.**

Ideas

✔ 1. Did you tell about one bird?

✔ 2. Did all your details tell about the topic?

Organization

✔ 3. Did you write a beginning, a middle, and an ending?

✔ 4. Did you include one main idea in each paragraph?

Sentence Fluency

✔ 5. Did you write complete sentences?

✔ 6. Did you use short and long sentences?

Tori's Revising

In part of her report, Tori made the following changes.

Two sentences are combined.

Exact words are added.

A Hummingbird has an interesting life cycle. The mother bird builds a small nest, ~~The mother bird builds it~~ out of tiny sticks and spiderwebs. She fills the nest with dandelion fluff and cattail fuzz. Then she lays two white eggs. The eggs are the size of peas.

When the chicks hatch, they are very tiny. The mother gathers ~~food~~ insects sap and nectar to feed her babies. They grow quickly.

Editing **Check your writing.**

When you edit, look at the following questions.

Edit ▶ **Use this checklist.**

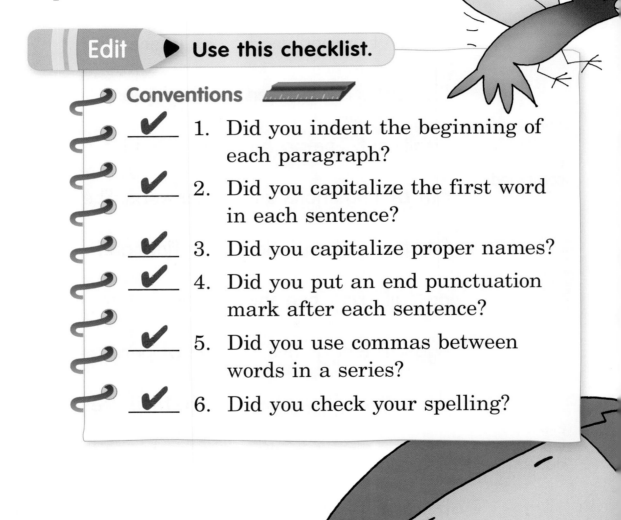

Conventions

___✔___ 1. Did you indent the beginning of each paragraph?

___✔___ 2. Did you capitalize the first word in each sentence?

___✔___ 3. Did you capitalize proper names?

___✔___ 4. Did you put an end punctuation mark after each sentence?

___✔___ 5. Did you use commas between words in a series?

___✔___ 6. Did you check your spelling?

Tori's Editing

In part of her report, Tori corrected the following mistakes.

A capitalization error is corrected.

A ~~H~~ummingbird has an interesting life cycle. The mother bird builds a small nest out of tiny sticks and spiderwebs. She fills the nest with dandelion fluff and cattail fuzz. Then she lays two white eggs. The eggs are the size of peas.

When the chicks hatch, they are very tiny. The mother gathers insects, sap, and nectar to feed her babies. They grow quickly.

Commas are added between words in a series.

Publishing **Create a title.**

Here are three ways to give your report a title.

1. Name your topic.

Hummingbirds

2. Describe your topic.

Tiny, Shiny Birds

3. Be creative.

Humming Wonders *

Here are three titles Tori wrote. She chose her favorite.

Publish ▶ **Create a title.**

1. List ideas for a title.
2. Choose your favorite.

Finish your report.

It is time to share your report. Tori was able to type her report into the computer. You can also neatly print your report.

Humming Wonders

A hummingbird is an amazing bird. When it flies, its wings go so fast that it hums. That is how it got its name. A hummingbird can fly up, down, forward, and even backward.

The hummingbird is tiny. It is about 3 1/2 inches long. Its feathers are mostly brown and gray, but some are a shiny green, purple, red, or orange.

Publish ▶ **Make a neat final copy.**

- Read your report to the class.
- Display it on the bulletin board.

Multimedia Presentation

Have you ever seen a slide show on a computer? Tori decided to turn her report into a slide show. It was a fun way to share her work with her class and with her grandma.

You can make a slide show with your report, too. This chapter will show you how.

Prewriting **Gather your details.**

Tori made a grid to plan her slide show. She made a slide for the main idea of each paragraph in her report.

Tori's Slide Grid

words on each slide	pictures	sounds	actions
1. Humming Wonders	hummingbird by flower	humming	flying bird
2. Birds are tiny and shiny.	big picture of a hummingbird	louder humming	bird flying up, down, forward, and backward

Prewrite ▶ **Create your grid.**

1. Set up your own grid. Number a row of boxes for each paragraph in your report.
2. Add ideas for pictures, sounds, and actions.

Writing **Make a storyboard.**

Next, Tori made a storyboard. A storyboard shows your plan for each slide in your presentation.

Part of Tori's Storyboard

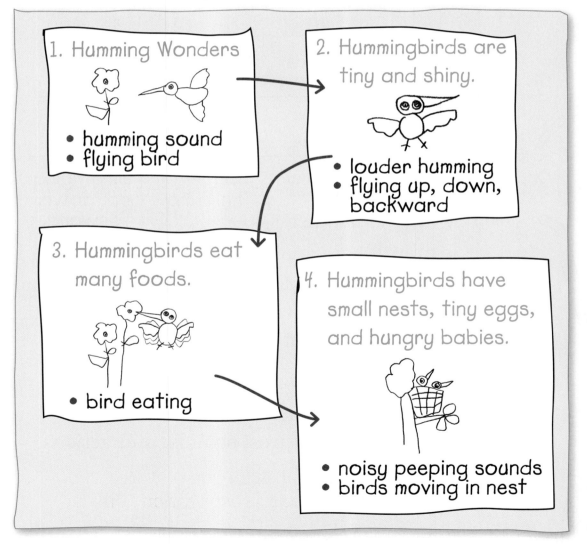

1. Humming Wonders
   - humming sound
   - flying bird

2. Hummingbirds are tiny and shiny.
   - louder humming
   - flying up, down, backward

3. Hummingbirds eat many foods.
   - bird eating

4. Hummingbirds have small nests, tiny eggs, and hungry babies.
   - noisy peeping sounds
   - birds moving in nest

Write ▶ Create your storyboard.

1. Set up six boxes, one for each slide.
2. Write words you want on each slide and add a drawing in each box.
3. Make an index card for each slide. Write out the information that you want to read while you show each slide.
4. Put your slides together on the computer.

Revise ▶ Improve your slide show.

5. Did you include all the important ideas?
6. Are your slides in the right order?

Edit ▶ Check your slides.

7. Are your words spelled correctly?
8. Did you use end punctuation?

Publish ▶ Present your slide show.

Practice reading your cards and showing your computer slides. Share your presentation with a partner or your family.

Speaking and Learning Skills

Dr. Martin Luther King, Jr., gave many great speeches. His most famous one is the "I Have a Dream" speech. People who listened to this speech never forgot it.

In this section, you will learn about making your own speeches. You will learn about listening and speaking to others. These skills will help you become a better student.

What's Ahead

- Giving Speeches
- Writing in Journals and Learning Logs
- Viewing and Listening Skills
- Taking Tests

Giving Speeches

Do you have a collection? Do you know how to make something? Have you just learned about an interesting topic?

You can share your special information in a classroom speech. Paco's speech is on the next page. After reading his speech, you will learn how to write your own.

Paco's Speech

Fool's Gold

When my family went to Colorado to visit my uncle, he gave me this rock. It's called pyrite. It's also called fool's gold.

Pyrite is shiny like real gold, but it is made of iron and sulfur. Pyrite is harder than gold. It makes sparks if you hit it. That's how it got its name. Pyrite means fire. Sometimes pyrite is made into jewelry. It's not as valuable as gold because it's easy to find.

Pyrite might be fool's gold, but it has real value to me. It's my favorite rock in my rock collection.

Prewriting Choose your topic.

Use one of these ideas below to help you select a topic.

Tell about something you like to do.

> I like to go fishing.

Tell about something you learned.

> I learned about Ruby Bridges.

Change a report you wrote into a speech.

> I wrote a report about fool's gold.

Know your purpose.

The **reason** you are giving the speech is called your **purpose.** Your purpose is to give information.

Prewrite ▶ **Choose your topic.**

1. Pick a topic for your speech.
2. Remember your purpose.

Prewriting **Gather your details.**

You can learn about your subject by remembering, reading, and asking questions.

> **Remember** List everything you already know about your topic.
>
> **Read** Learn more about the topic.
>
> **Ask Questions** Interview someone who knows about your topic.

Plan your speech.

In the **Beginning** of your speech, name your topic and catch your listeners' attention.

In the **Middle** of your speech, list the main facts about your topic.

In the **Ending** of your speech, share why the topic is important to you.

Writing Create your speech.

Paco used index cards to make notes.

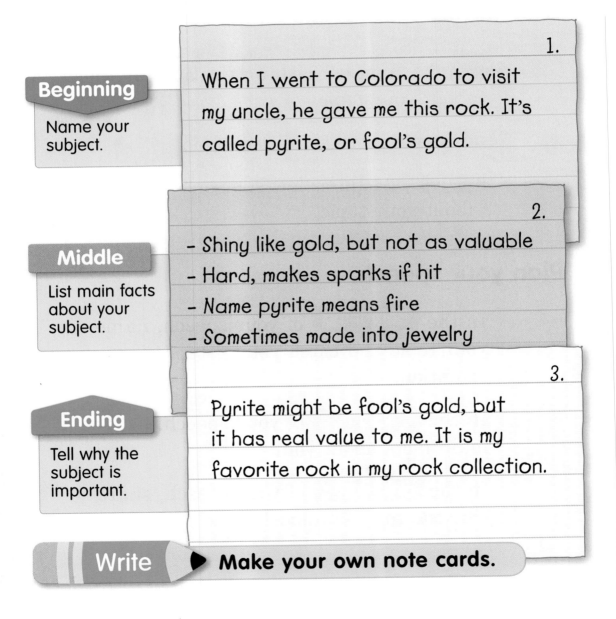

Beginning

Name your subject.

> 1.
>
> When I went to Colorado to visit my uncle, he gave me this rock. It's called pyrite, or fool's gold.

Middle

List main facts about your subject.

> 2.
>
> - Shiny like gold, but not as valuable
> - Hard, makes sparks if hit
> - Name pyrite means fire
> - Sometimes made into jewelry

Ending

Tell why the subject is important.

> 3.
>
> Pyrite might be fool's gold, but it has real value to me. It is my favorite rock in my rock collection.

Write ▶ **Make your own note cards.**

Publishing Give your speech.

Once you finish your note cards or writing out your speech, it's time to get ready for your audience.

Practice giving your talk.

1. If you are using **note cards**, practice sharing the ideas listed on each card.
2. Say your speech over and over, so you almost know it by heart.
3. If you wrote out your speech word for word, practice reading it until you almost have it memorized.
4. As you practice, think of visual aids to share. You can show a picture, a chart, or an object related to your topic.

Publish ▶ Give your speech.

1. Look at your audience.
2. Speak slowly, clearly, and loudly.
3. Relax, smile, and enjoy giving your speech.

Writing in
Journals and Learning Logs

Most authors keep **journals** for writing down things they learn. Keeping a journal gives them ideas for writing.

This chapter will show you how to keep your own journal. It will also tell you about learning logs.

Keep a personal journal.

A **personal journal** is your own special writing place. You can write about things that happen to you and things you wonder about. Miki went on a field trip with her class. She wrote about it in her journal.

Miki's Journal Entry

January 18, 2006

My class went to the Garden Domes. It felt like summer inside the domes. The flowers were pretty. The air smelled sweet. There were birds singing and flying around everywhere! I think I'll dream about summer tonight!

Practice

1. Start your personal journal.
2. Begin by writing the date at the top.
3. Write about what you did or something that happened.

Write in a reading journal.

A **reading journal** is a place to write about the books you read.

You can write about

- how you felt about the book
- your favorite part
- your favorite character
- something you learned

Jamal's Journal Entry

In his journal, Jamal told how he felt about a folktale.

March 30, 2006

The drawings in <u>The Paper Crane</u> are really cool. The story is about folded paper cranes. I want to make cranes out of paper, too.

Practice

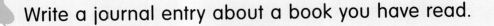

Write a journal entry about a book you have read.

Write in a learning log.

Your teacher may want you to write in a **learning log**. It helps you learn more.

Katie's Science Entry

Katie wrote about what she learned in her science class.

September 21, 2006

Today we experimented with compasses. We learned that a compass has a magnet inside that points north. That's because the North Pole has a magnetic pull.

Practice

Write a learning log entry about something you learned in science. Draw a picture, too.

Viewing and Listening Skills

Every day you learn new things in school and at home. You can also learn many interesting things from certain types of TV programs.

This chapter will help you become a smarter viewer of TV specials, regular programs, and commercials. You'll even learn about viewing Web sites.

View news programs.

News programs report important information. These programs tell what is happening in your community, across the country, and around the world.

A **news story** includes the most important facts and details about an event. The facts in a news story should answer the 5 W questions. Jacob watched a news story, and then he answered the 5 W's.

Sample Local News Story

Who?	a wheelchair basketball team
What?	will play a game
Where?	at the high school
When?	Saturday afternoon
Why?	to raise money for the team

Talk it over.

1. Watch a news story with an adult.

2. Listen for answers to the 5 W's.

3. Did the news story answer all of the questions?

View TV specials.

TV specials can be about anything—giraffes, firefighters, weather, or other subjects. Raul watched a special about talking drums.

Before viewing

Raul wrote questions about the subject.

During viewing

Raul wrote key words to answer his questions.

Questions	Answers
What are talking drums?	drums with long strings
Where do people use them?	Africa
Why do people use them?	send messages

After viewing

Raul wrote about the program. He listed important ideas and drew a picture to help him remember the information.

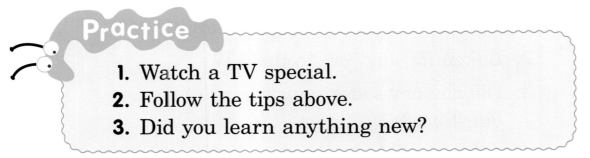

Practice

1. Watch a TV special.
2. Follow the tips above.
3. Did you learn anything new?

Raul's Response to a TV Special

November 11

I watched a TV show about talking drums. People in Africa use these drums. Drummers send messages to each other. They make high and low sounds by pulling the drum's strings. The sounds stand for different words and feelings. The messages tell about being happy, excited, or scared. This is what the drum looks like.

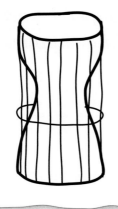

Understand commercials.

Have you noticed that most **TV commercials** are louder than TV programs are? That's because commercials are made to get your attention. Most of them try to get you to buy something. You need your best viewing skills as you watch them.

Two Selling Methods: Here are two ways commercials try to sell products.

Be just like a famous person.

Melinda Lou is a fast swimmer because she takes a Swifty vitamin each day. You should take Swifty vitamins, too.

Join the crowd.

Everyone is buying the newest Super Duper Scooter. Hurry, buy one now while supplies last.

Practice

Become an expert viewer.
1. Study a few commercials.
2. Do they use either of the selling methods above?

View Web sites.

Web sites can link you to people and places all over the world. That means you can learn about any topic. By following the tips below, you can find good information.

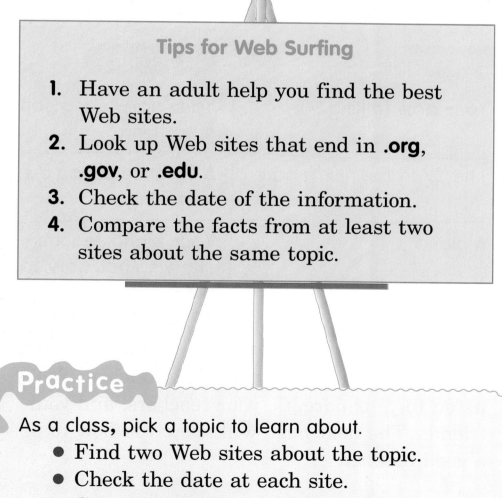

Tips for Web Surfing

1. Have an adult help you find the best Web sites.
2. Look up Web sites that end in **.org**, **.gov**, or **.edu**.
3. Check the date of the information.
4. Compare the facts from at least two sites about the same topic.

Practice

As a class, pick a topic to learn about.
- Find two Web sites about the topic.
- Check the date at each site.
- Compare the facts on the two sites.

Learn to listen.

What's the difference between listening and hearing? Hearing is when your ears take in sound, like the bell ringing. Listening is when you pay attention to what you hear. When you think about directions your teacher gives, you're listening.

Hearing	Listening
Your mom talking	Your mom telling you something
The TV in the next room	A TV special you are watching
A piano	Your piano teacher showing you how to play a song

Tune In Listening is a great way to learn. You listen to your parents, your teachers, and your friends. The next page will show you how to be a good listener.

Good Listener Checklist

✔ 1. Look at the speaker. Watch the speaker's face and hands.

✔ 2. Listen for key words. They help you remember information.

✔ 3. Listen to directions. They tell you what to do.

✔ 4. Ask questions. When you don't understand, ask for help.

When you become a good listener, you will learn a lot more.

Taking Tests

In school you stay busy. You learn about new things and practice new skills. You make things. Then you take tests!

Tests are important because they help you and your teacher know if you understand what you are studying.

Test-Taking Tips

Here are some tips to follow when you take a test.

- **Write** your name on the top of your paper.

- **Listen** to all the directions your teacher gives.

- **Ask** questions if you do not understand something.

- **Answer** the questions you are sure of first.

- **Skip** the ones you are not sure of.

- Then **go back** and answer any questions you skipped.

- **Check** all your answers.

Multiple-Choice Test

In a **multiple-choice test**, you may have a list of sentences to complete. Your job is to pick the best choice to complete each sentence. Here are some tips.

- Read the sentence using each choice.
- Then reread the sentence with your best choice.
- Be sure your choice makes sense.

Sample

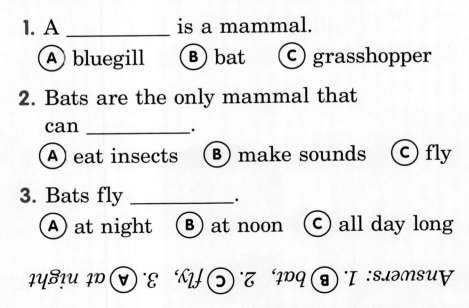

Directions: Fill in the circle in front of the word that best completes each sentence.

1. A _____ is a mammal.
   (A) bluegill   (B) bat   (C) grasshopper

2. Bats are the only mammal that can _____.
   (A) eat insects   (B) make sounds   (C) fly

3. Bats fly _____.
   (A) at night   (B) at noon   (C) all day long

Answers: 1. (B) bat, 2. (C) fly, 3. (A) at night

Matching Test

A **matching test** has two lists of words. You must match each word in the first list with a word in the second list. Here are some tips.

- Start with the first word in the left column.
- Read the words in the right column to find a word that matches.
- Make neat lines to match the words.

Sample

Directions: Draw a line from each word in column A to the word with the opposite meaning in column B.

A	B
dark	soft
sharp	light
hard	dull

Answers: dark-light, sharp-dull, hard-soft

Fill-in-the-Blanks Test

A **fill-in-the-blanks test** gives you a list of sentences to finish. You write the correct word or words on the blank lines. Here are some tips.

- Read each sentence carefully.
- Choose a word from the Word Bank.
- Read the sentence with the word in it.
- If the word makes sense, write it.

Sample

Directions: Look at the picture and read each sentence. Then find a word in the Word Bank to complete each sentence. Write the word on the line.

Word Bank
gas   liquid   solid

1. The hot chocolate is a _____.

2. The hot chocolate's steam is a _____.

3. The mug is a _____.

Answers: 1. liquid 2. gas 3. solid

Short-Answer Test

In a **short-answer test**, you write answers in complete sentences. Here are some tips.

- Read each question carefully.
- Ask questions if you don't understand something.
- Answer the question in one or two complete sentences.

Sample

Directions: Write complete sentences to answer each of the following questions.

1. Who lives in the White House?

   The president of the United States lives in the White House.

2. What does the American flag look like?

   The American flag has red and white stripes. It also has a blue box with 50 white stars inside.

Words and Sentences

Do you remember playing with blocks? Maybe you liked to make forts with them. Or maybe you built little houses or tall towers. Words are just like building blocks. They're fun to play with, and you can build all kinds of sentences with them. This section will help you use words to build terrific sentences.

What's Ahead

Working with Words

Do you know how many words there are in the English language? There are thousands and thousands of them! You already use a lot of these words. And you will learn many more as you read new books and study new subjects.

In this chapter you will learn about nouns, pronouns, verbs, adjectives, and adverbs.

Annie

Mini Index

Learning About Nouns

A **noun** is a word that names a person, place, or thing.

Annie walked to the store to buy an orange.

person   place   thing

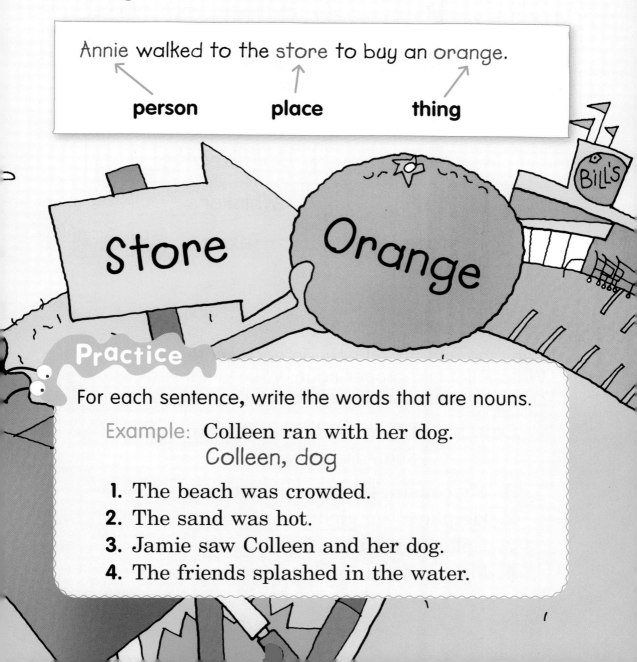

Store   Orange

Practice

For each sentence, write the words that are nouns.

Example: Colleen ran with her dog.
Colleen, dog

1. The beach was crowded.
2. The sand was hot.
3. Jamie saw Colleen and her dog.
4. The friends splashed in the water.

Common and Proper Nouns

A **common noun** names any person, place, or thing. A **proper noun** names a special person, place, or thing. Proper nouns always begin with capital letters.

Common Nouns	Proper Nouns
girl	Lina
street	Oak Street
cat	Whiskers
state	Texas

Practice

Copy the underlined noun in each sentence below. Write *P* if it is a proper noun. Write *C* if it is a common noun. Capitalize the proper nouns.

Example: I flew with Mom to <u>sun valley</u>.
Sun Valley, P

1. My cousin, <u>thomas</u>, lives there.
2. He plays the <u>violin</u>.
3. I played with his dog, <u>bowser</u>.
4. My cousin is coming here next <u>year</u>.

Singular and Plural Nouns

Nouns can be singular or plural. **Singular** means *one*. **Plural** means *more than one*. To make most nouns plural, add **-s** at the end of the word.

Singular Nouns	Plural Nouns
coat	coats
rabbit	rabbits
girl	girls

Practice

Copy the underlined noun in each sentence below. Write *S* if the noun is singular and *PL* if it is plural.

Example: Mike and Andi opened their <u>eyes</u>.
eyes, PL

1. They saw two new <u>bikes</u>.
2. Andi put on her <u>jacket</u>.
3. Mike quickly put on his <u>shoes</u>.
4. The twins took a <u>ride</u>.

Nouns That End in -es

To form the plural of a noun that ends with **sh**, **ch**, **x**, **s**, and **z**, add **-es** to the end of the word.

Singular Nouns	Plural Nouns
wish	wishes
bunch	bunches
box	boxes
dress	dresses
buzz	buzzes

Practice

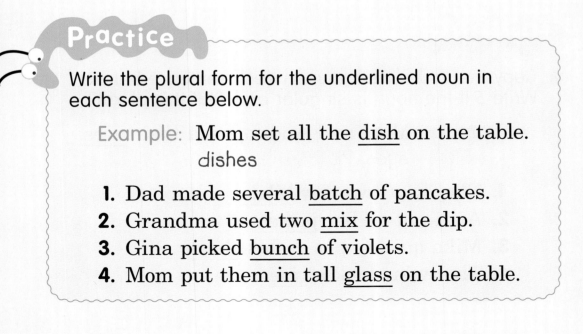

Write the plural form for the underlined noun in each sentence below.

Example: Mom set all the <u>dish</u> on the table.
dishes

1. Dad made several <u>batch</u> of pancakes.
2. Grandma used two <u>mix</u> for the dip.
3. Gina picked <u>bunch</u> of violets.
4. Mom put them in tall <u>glass</u> on the table.

Nouns That End in y

To form the plural of many nouns that end in **y**, remember this rule.

Change the **y** to **i** and add **-es**.

lady ⟶ ladi + es = ladies

Singular Nouns	Plural Nouns
puppy	puppies
penny	pennies
jelly	jellies
story	stories

Practice

Use the rule above to write the plural of each noun below. Then use each plural noun in a sentence.

Example: country ⟶ countries
       Dad travels to many countries.

1. party   3. baby
2. pony   4. city

Possessive Nouns

A **possessive noun** shows ownership. To make a singular noun possessive, place an **'s** at the end of the word. To form most plural possessives, add the apostrophe (**'**) at the end of the word.

Have you seen <u>Bobbi's</u> hamster?
(The hamster belongs to Bobbi.)

We followed the <u>rabbits'</u> tracks.
(The tracks belong to more
than one rabbit.)

Practice

For each sentence, write the possessive noun.

Example: Our neighbor's car is orange.
neighbor's

1. Mr. Lee's dog is friendly.
2. That bicycle's tire is flat.
3. The school's doors were just painted.
4. The boys' softball gloves got wet.

How can I use nouns?

You can use **clear nouns** to give the reader a better picture of what you mean. If you use the word *flower*, it means any flower. But if you use the word *tulip*, your reader knows exactly what you mean.

General Noun	Clear Noun
neighbor	Mr. Cosfa
park	Central Park
building	firehouse
dog	terrier
tree	maple

Practice

For each general noun below, write a clear noun.

Example: teacher
         Ms. Daniels

1. shoe
2. friend
3. store
4. bird
5. snack

Using Pronouns

A **pronoun** is a word that takes the place of a noun. Here are some common pronouns.

I	he	she	we	they	you
me	him	her	us	them	it

Look at how the pronoun replaces the nouns in the sentence below.

Claudia and Stella   jump rope.

They   jump rope.

Practice

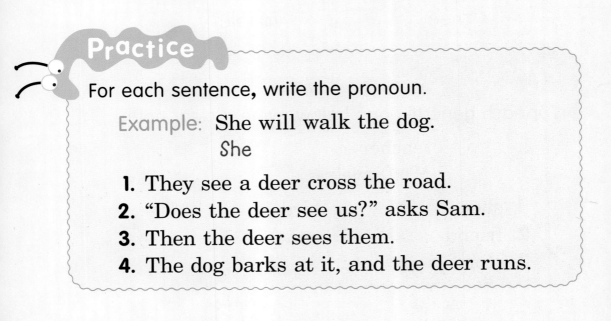

For each sentence, write the pronoun.

Example: She will walk the dog.
She

1. They see a deer cross the road.
2. "Does the deer see us?" asks Sam.
3. Then the deer sees them.
4. The dog barks at it, and the deer runs.

Singular and Plural Pronouns

Pronouns are **singular** and **plural** just like nouns. Remember that singular means *one* and plural means *more than one.*

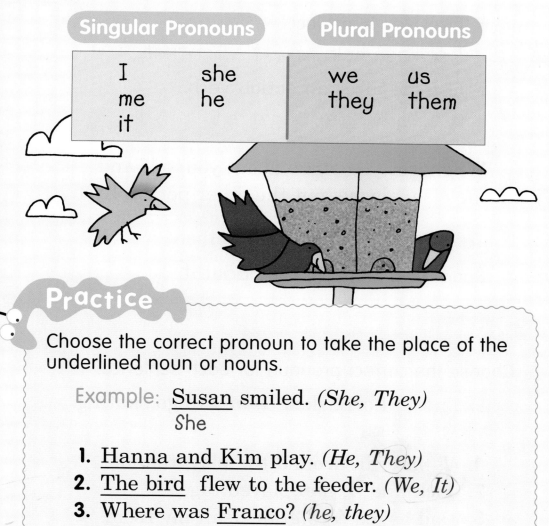

Singular Pronouns		Plural Pronouns	
I	she	we	us
me	he	they	them
it			

Practice

Choose the correct pronoun to take the place of the underlined noun or nouns.

Example: <u>Susan</u> smiled. *(She, They)*
She

1. <u>Hanna and Kim</u> play. *(He, They)*
2. <u>The bird</u> flew to the feeder. *(We, It)*
3. Where was <u>Franco</u>? *(he, they)*
4. <u>Theresa</u> swims well. *(She, He)*

Using *I* and *Me*

When you write about yourself, use the singular pronoun **I** or **me**. The word **I** is always capitalized.

- Use **I** as a subject.
  I always help my little brother.

- Use **me** after an action verb.
  Fran gave me the letter.

Whenever you write about yourself and someone else, always put the other person first.

Tam and I are working together.

Sandi told Mom and me about it.

Practice

Choose the correct pronoun for each sentence.

Example: Lori asked (*I, me*) to go skating.
me

1. (*I, me*) ran around the playground.
2. Jack and (*I, me*) played tag.
3. Dad asked (*I, me*) to clean my room.
4. Tom told Mom and (*I, me*) about the trip.

Using *We* and *Us*

When you write about yourself and others, use the plural pronouns **we** and **us**.

- Use **we** as the subject of a sentence.

  We are going to the school picnic.

- Use **us** after an action verb.

  Mr. Tylor asked us a question.

Practice

Choose either *we* or *us* for each sentence below.

Example: Please give _____ the invitations.

     us

1. _____ will plan the party together.

2. Mom and Dad always give _____ snacks.

3. _____ want to make the decorations.

4. Please tell _____ what to do next.

Possessive Pronouns

A **possessive pronoun** shows who or what owns something. It takes the place of a possessive noun.

> my   his   her   its   our   their

Possessive Nouns	Possessive Pronouns
Devon's mitt	his mitt
Jenna's class	her class
Tom and Bina's pictures	their pictures
the book's cover	its cover

Practice

Choose the correct pronoun for each underlined possessive noun below.

Example: That is <u>Dee and Jen's</u> house.
(*their, her*)
their

1. Did you find <u>Olivia's</u> locket? (*her, its*)
2. Mom saw <u>Leon's</u> hat. (*her, his*)
3. This is <u>Jake and Ron's</u> room. (*their, his*)
4. We fixed <u>the bike's</u> tire. (*its, his*)

How can I use pronouns?

Pronouns can be used to form contractions. A **contraction** is a shortened word made from two words. An apostrophe **(')** shows that one or more letters are left out.

Pronoun	+	Verb	=	Contraction
he	+	is	=	he's
she	+	is	=	she's
it	+	is	=	it's
you	+	are	=	you're
we	+	are	=	we're
they	+	are	=	they're

Practice

Write the contraction for each set of words in the sentences below.

Example: *(They are)* planting a garden.
They're

1. I think *(it is)* almost time to go home.
2. Coach Lee says *(you are)* a good pitcher.
3. *(He is)* our neighbor.
4. Mom said *(we are)* going on a trip!

Learning About Verbs

A **verb** usually tells what is happening in a sentence.

Action Verbs

An **action verb** tells what action is being done.

> The kangaroo <u>hops</u>.
> Ravi <u>jumps</u>.
> Lin <u>sings</u>.

Practice

Write the action verb from each sentence below.

Example: We clean our desks.
           clean

1. The rain pounds the sidewalk.
2. Little frogs leap in the grass.
3. The trees bend in the wind.
4. We hear thunder.
5. I love summer storms.

Helping Verbs

   Helping verbs come before the main verb. They help to show action or time. Here are some common helping verbs.

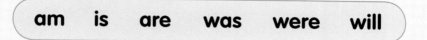

am   is   are   was   were   will

> He is running in a race.
> (*Is* helps the main verb *running*.)
>
> We were reading that story in class.
> (*Were* helps the main verb *reading*.)

Practice

Write the helping verb and the main verb from each sentence below.

   Example: I am playing at Katie's house.
          am playing

   1. We are making a scrapbook.
   2. I am finding pictures for the pages.
   3. Katie was looking for decorations.
   4. She is collecting buttons and ribbons.
   5. Katie and I will use markers and crayons.

Linking Verbs

Linking verbs complete a thought. The following *be* verbs can be linking verbs.

> am   is   are   was   were

I am hungry.

My cat is very pretty.

Sam and Dana are friends.

Lani was a funny girl.

We were lost.

Practice

Write a sentence for each of the linking verbs below. Underline the linking verb in each of your sentences.

Example: were

We <u>were</u> late for school.

1. am   **3.** are   **5.** were

2. is   **4.** was

Verb Tenses

A verb's tense tells when the action happens. The action can happen in the **present**, in the **past**, or in the **future**.

present tense—The action is happening.	Andy skates with his friends.
past tense—The action did happen.	Andy skated with his friends yesterday.
future tense—The action will happen.	Andy will skate with his friends tomorrow.

Practice

Write a sentence for each of the verbs below. Then tell the tense of each verb.

Example: visited
Owen visited the Grand Canyon last year.
past

1. plays
2. will bake
3. dropped
4. reads

How can I use verbs correctly with nouns?

Your verbs will be correct if your subject and verb **agree in number**. That means a singular subject uses a singular verb, and a plural subject uses a plural verb.

Singular Subject Noun and Singular Verb	Plural Subject Noun and Plural Verb
Juan . . . laughs. cleans. dives. sleeps.	The boys . . . laugh. clean. dive. sleep.

Practice

For each sentence below, write the verb that agrees with the subject.

Example: Lucy *(play, plays)* in the band.

plays

1. The children *(draw, draws)* pictures.
2. Gabe *(read, reads)* comic books.
3. Jon *(ride, rides)* his bike after school.
4. My friends *(play, plays)* chess.

How can **I** use verbs correctly with pronouns?

When a pronoun is used as a subject, it should **agree in number** with the verb. Look at the chart below.

Singular Subject Pronoun and Singular Verb	Plural Subject Pronoun and Plural Verb
He <u>likes</u> snow.	They <u>like</u> snow.
She <u>wants</u> help.	They <u>want</u> help.
It <u>drinks</u> water.	They <u>drink</u> water.

Practice

For each sentence below, write the verb that agrees with the subject.

Example: We (*go, goes*) to the park.

go

1. They (*find, finds*) a lost dog.
2. It (*wag, wags*) its tail!
3. She (*want, wants*) to find the owners.
4. They (*make, makes*) a lost-and-found poster.
5. He (*is, are*) happy to see Spot again.

Working with Adjectives

An **adjective** is a word that describes a noun.

Adjectives tell what kind.

Adjectives that tell **what kind** are very important. They make writing fun to read.

> The **huge** owls flew away.
> The dog chased the **yellow** ball.
> We heard **loud** music outside.

Practice

For each sentence below, find the adjective that tells what kind.

Example: Let's visit the brick building.
brick

1. The building has a round dome.
2. A squeaky fan cools me.
3. I ate a spicy burrito.
4. My old quilt keeps me warm.
5. We played in the white sand.

Adjectives tell which one.

Adjectives that tell **which one** help make your writing clear.

> **this**   **that**   **these**   **those**

This book is very exciting.

I want to read **that** book again.

Did you hear **those** stories?

These pictures are my favorites.

Practice

For each sentence below, find the adjective that tells which one.

Example: This book shows the moon
          landing.
          This

1. Grandpa remembers that day.
2. Those astronauts were brave.
3. Grandpa gave me these pictures.
4. This photo shows the moon.
5. Just look at those craters!

Adjectives tell how many.

Some adjectives tell you **how many**.

> **one** tree   **four** birds   **two** pages
> We bought **three** tickets.

Practice

Write a sentence for each adjective below.

Example: one
Winslow School has one gym.

1. two   **2.** three   **3.** four   **4.** five

Articles

A, an, and *the* are special adjectives called **articles**. Use *a* before words that begin with a consonant. Use *an* before words that begin with a vowel.

> a lamb   an octopus   the zoo

Practice

Write one sentence using *a,* one sentence using *an,* and one sentence using *the.*

How can I use adjectives?

You can use adjectives to **compare** two people, places, or things. To compare *two* nouns, add **-er** to the end of the adjective.

> The yellow car is smaller than the green car.

To compare *three or more* nouns, add **-est** to the end of the adjective.

> The blue car is the smallest one of all.

Practice

In each sentence below, choose the correct adjective.

> Example: I am (*older, oldest*) than Tim.
> older

1. He is the (*younger, youngest*) boy in class.
2. Danni is a (*faster, fastest*) runner than I am.
3. She is the (*taller, tallest*) girl I know.
4. Your chair is (*softer, softest*) than mine.
5. Joe caught a (*bigger, biggest*) fish than Ryan caught.

Learning About Adverbs

An **adverb** is a word that describes a verb. It answers **when**, **where**, or **how** an action happens.

> It rained yesterday. (When?)
>
> We ran inside. (Where?)
>
> The thunder rumbled loudly. (How?)

Practice

For each sentence below, write the adverb that answers the asking word in (parentheses).

Example: Grandpa and I went fishing today.
(When?)
today

1. We sat quietly. *(How?)*
2. The fish swam quickly. *(How?)*
3. I let my hook sink down. *(Where?)*
4. A bluegill finally grabbed the bait. *(When?)*
5. I carefully put the fish back in the water. *(How?)*

How can I use adverbs?

You can use adverbs to make your writing clear. The adverbs in the following sentences answer **how**.

Roy slowly poured the water.

Maria proudly read her report.

The snow fell softly.

Practice

Write each sentence below, using the adverb in parentheses that you like best.

Example: The snake slithered (*silently, quickly*).

The snake slithered silently.

1. Otters swim (*smoothly, gracefully*).
2. Prairie dogs (*quickly, always*) pop out of their holes.
3. Monkeys (*carefully, cleverly*) peel bananas.
4. Woodpeckers (*noisily, sometimes*) peck trees.

Writing
Sentences

Sentences come in all sizes. Some are very long. Others are quite short. No matter what their size, every sentence must tell a complete thought. Every sentence also begins with a capital letter and ends with a punctuation mark. In this chapter, you will learn all about sentences.

Mini Index

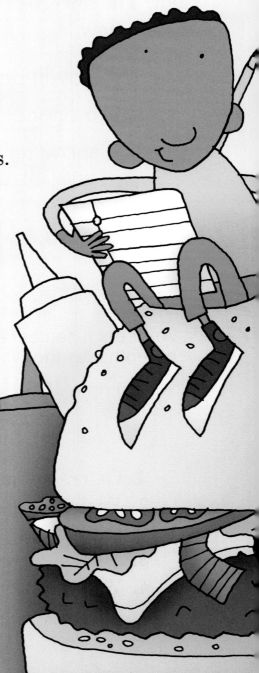

Writing Complete Sentences
Correct Word Order

The words in a sentence must be in the correct order to make sense. The group of words below does not make sense.

> hamburger Billy eats a lunch for

If you put these words in the correct order, they tell a complete, clear thought.

> Billy eats a hamburger for lunch.

Practice

Put the groups of words below in the correct order to make sentences. Remember that a sentence starts with a capital letter and ends with a punctuation mark.

Example: is hamburger the hot
The hamburger is hot.

1. pickles puts hamburger on his Billy
2. squirts his on ketchup hamburger he
3. a little likes also he mustard

Subject of a Sentence

The **naming part** of a sentence is called the **subject**. The subject tells who or what the sentence is about.

Ms. Davis is our teacher. She walks to school.

Ms. Davis is the subject of the first sentence. **She** is the subject of the second sentence.

Practice

Write the subject of each sentence below.

Example: The school is near our teacher's house.
The school

1. The house has a big porch.
2. Students walk past her house.
3. Parents wave to Ms. Davis.
4. The crossing guard helps the students.
5. Students carry the teacher's book bag.

Predicate of a Sentence

The **telling part** of the sentence is called the **predicate**. It tells what the subject does. The predicate always includes a verb.

Crickets chirp loudly.

Chirp loudly is the predicate. It tells what the crickets do. The word **chirp** is the verb.

> # Chirp!

Practice

Write the predicate of each sentence below.

Example: Crickets look like grasshoppers.
look like grasshoppers

1. Many crickets hide during the day.
2. Crickets live on trees.
3. They move slowly in cold weather.
4. Field crickets eat grass and wood.
5. Some people keep crickets as pets.

Fixing Sentence Problems

Sentence Fragments

Every sentence needs a subject and a predicate to make sense. A **sentence fragment** is missing a subject or a predicate (verb).

Fragment	Sentence
Sleeps under a tree. (The subject is missing.)	The dog sleeps under a tree. (A subject is added.)
The dog around the yard. (The verb is missing.)	The dog runs around the yard. (A verb is added.)

Practice

The sentence fragments below are missing a subject or a verb. Make each one a sentence.

Example: Ranger loudly.

Ranger barks loudly.

1. Loves playing in the park.
2. Other dogs after him.
3. Ranger once into the pond.

Rambling Sentences

A **rambling sentence** is one that goes on and on. Try not to use the word *and* too many times.

Rambling Sentence:

My mother told me to get some milk and I went to the dairy section and I looked for a gallon carton and I finally found it.

Better Sentences:

My mother told me to get some milk. I went to the dairy section and looked for a gallon carton. I finally found it.

Practice

Rewrite this rambling sentence. Turn it into three or four sentences by taking out some of the *and*'s.

Joanie calls her friends and she asks them to go to the park and they have fun swinging and they have fun sliding.

Subject-Verb Agreement

Subjects and verbs must agree in number. A singular subject must have a singular verb. A plural subject must have a plural verb.

Bob has a silver wheelchair.
(The subject and the verb are singular.)

Two other boys have red wheelchairs.
(The subject and the verb are plural.)

Practice

Write the verb that agrees with the subject for each sentence below.

Example: Bob (go, goes) to Cooper School.
goes

1. Justin (push, pushes) Bob's wheelchair.
2. Justin and Bob (is, are) good friends.
3. Bob (is, are) eight years old.
4. Bob (tell, tells) funny stories.
5. His friends always (laugh, laughs).

Using Different Kinds of Sentences

There are four kinds of sentences.

A **telling** sentence makes a statement.

You have a box of crayons.

An **asking** sentence asks a question.

Do you have a red crayon?

A **command** sentence makes a request or gives directions.

Please put your crayons away.

An **exclamatory** sentence shows surprise or strong feelings.

Your crayons are going to fall!

Practice

Write what kind of sentence each one is.

Example: Crayons are made in many colors.
            telling

1. How many crayons do you have?
2. I love your drawing!
3. Please pass me the blue crayon.
4. I want to draw the ocean.

Combining Short Sentences

Sometimes, short sentences have the same subject. These sentences can be combined to make one longer sentence.

Short Sentences:

Jerry gets dressed. Jerry eats breakfast.

Combined:

Jerry gets dressed and eats breakfast.

The word **and** is used to combine the sentences.

Practice

Combine these short sentences to make longer sentences.

Example: The store buys fresh peaches.
The store sells fresh peaches.
The store buys and sells fresh peaches.

1. The school bus stops.
   The school bus picks up three students.
2. Jenna's friends talk.
   Jenna's friends laugh.
3. Kenny sits down at his desk.
   Kenny opens his book.

You can also combine short sentences that have the same predicate.

Short Sentences:

Ellen cleaned the board.
Lila cleaned the board.

Combined:

Ellen and Lila cleaned the board.

The word **and** is used to combine the sentences.

Practice

Combine these short sentences to make longer sentences. (You may need to change a singular verb to a plural verb in your new sentence.)

Example: Sam reads a lot.
Paula reads a lot.

Sam and Paula read a lot.

1. Sharon jumps rope during recess.
Jill jumps rope during recess.

2. Ryan learns about question marks.
Thomas learns about question marks.

3. The girls like the goldfish.
The boys like the goldfish.

Practice Test

On your own paper, write the letter that answers each question.

1. Which sentence is a fragment?
  a. The movie lasts two hours.
  b. Bryan all the way home.
  c. It is time for lunch.

2. Which sentence puts the following group of words in the correct order?

old eight today is years Bobby
  a. Today is eight years old Bobby.
  b. Old today is eight years Bobby.
  c. Bobby is eight years old today.

3. What is the subject of this sentence?

George looks at the stars.
  a. the stars
  b. looks
  c. George

4. What is the predicate of this sentence?

Russell sets the table.
  a. sets the table
  b. sets the
  c. Russell

5. What kind of sentence is this?

Do you have a favorite book?

    a. a telling sentence
    b. an asking sentence
    c. an exclamatory sentence

6. Which choice correctly combines these two short sentences?

Barb plays soccer.
Jo plays soccer.

    a. Jo plays soccer. Barb plays soccer.
    b. Barb plays soccer and Jo.
    c. Barb and Jo play soccer.

7. Which choice correctly combines these two sentences?

Sean hits the ball.
Sean runs to first base.

    a. Sean hits and runs the ball to first base.
    b. Sean hits the ball and runs to first base.
    c. Sean runs to first base. Sean hits the ball.

A Writer's Resource

Writing can feel like a very big job. Do you need help getting started? Are you looking for a writing topic? Are you trying to put your ideas in order or think of the right word to use? Wherever you are in the writing process, turn to these pages for help.

What's Ahead

How can I find a good topic?

Keep a writer's notebook.

Good writing ideas are everywhere. Keep a list of ideas in a notebook. Someday you may use these ideas in a story, a letter, a report, or even in a poem.

Write about what is going on around you.

You may see something interesting right in your own backyard.

Sample Writer's Notebook

A big gray squirrel is sitting on a bird feeder. How did it get up there? A red bird wants to come to the feeder. That squirrel is scaring the birds and throwing seeds all over!

List topics in your notebook.

List interesting people, places, and things in your writer's notebook. Then look over your lists when you need writing ideas.

Sample Writer's Notebook

People	Places	Things
teacher	school	car
pilot	home	bike
doctor	Ohio	lion
parent	library	desk
brother	zoo	game

Finish sentence starters.

Your teacher may give you some sentence starters. You may also think of your own. Add them to your notebook.

Sample Writer's Notebook

I like to . . .

I laugh when . . .

Stormy days . . .

My teacher says we need . . .

Dogs bark because . . .

I sing . . .

Keep a reading journal.

Read, read, read. Books and magazines are full of ideas. Keep a reading journal to write about what you learn in your reading.

Sample Reading Journal Entry

March 21, 2006

Today I read about manatees. They are also called sea cows. They eat water plants just like cows eat grass! They look as big as a walrus and move very slowly. Maybe I can see them in Florida someday.

How can I find more writing ideas?

Think about the basics-of-life words.

Look at the basics-of-life words to get topic ideas. Each category word reminds you of what people need to live.

Shelter   **Food**   **Clothing**

Sample Writing Idea

I choose the word shelter. That makes me think of an igloo. I could write about how an igloo is made.

Animals   **Family**   **Friends**

Sample Writing Idea

I choose the word friends. That makes me think of Erin and Sarah. I could write a story about making new friends in my new school.

How can I find special topics?

Here are topic ideas for each form of writing.

For **descriptive** writing, you could **describe** . . .
People: a sister, a cousin, an aunt, a teacher
Places: your room, the lunchroom, a library
Things: a toy, a hat, a tree, an octopus

For **narrative** writing, you could **tell what happened** . . .
during a ride on the bus
on your first day of school
in a funny dream

For **expository** writing, you could **explain** . . .
how to fly a kite
why you like to draw
information about eagles

For **persuasive** writing, you could **convince** your reader to . . .
be polite on a field trip
eat a good breakfast
read a special book

How do I write topic sentences?

Know your purpose.

You write to describe, to share a story, to explain, or to convince someone. The reason for your writing is called your **purpose**. A topic sentence lets the reader know the main idea of the paragraph.

Purpose: To Describe

Descriptive writing shows the reader a topic.

The red race car sounds like a jet plane.

Purpose: To Share a Story

Narrative writing tells a story.

Yesterday, my brother broke his arm.

Purpose: To Explain Something

Expository writing shares information.

Giving a dog a bath is a big job.

Purpose: To Convince Someone

Persuasive writing tries to get the reader to agree with an opinion.

A turtle makes a great pet.

How can I organize my ideas?

Use graphic organizers.

When you play softball, you follow a plan. First, you and your friends choose sides. Then you set up the field with bases. When you write, you also need a plan. A graphic organizer helps you plan your writing. Look at the graphic organizers on pages **359–365**.

List steps in a sequence chart.

Use a **sequence chart** to put details in order. Then when you begin writing, your details will be in the right order.

Sequence Chart

Topic	How to Bake Bread
First	Find the ingredients.
Next	Mix the ingredients.
Then	Turn on the oven.
Last	Bake the ingredients.

Compare topics with a Venn diagram.

Use a **Venn diagram** when you compare two topics. In spaces 1 and 2, list how the topics are different. In space 3, list how the topics are alike.

Venn Diagram

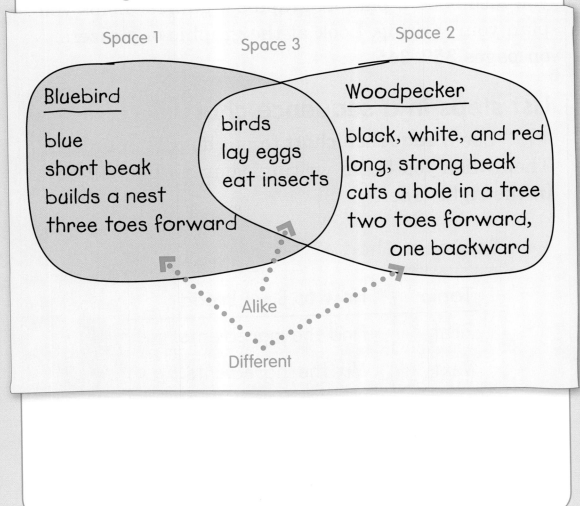

Space 1   Space 3   Space 2

Bluebird

blue
short beak
builds a nest
three toes forward

birds
lay eggs
eat insects

Woodpecker

black, white, and red
long, strong beak
cuts a hole in a tree
two toes forward,
          one backward

Alike

Different

Gather details with a cluster.

Make a **cluster**, also called a **web**, to help you think about your topic. Write your topic in the middle of your paper. Draw a circle around it. Then write as many ideas as you can about your topic.

Cluster

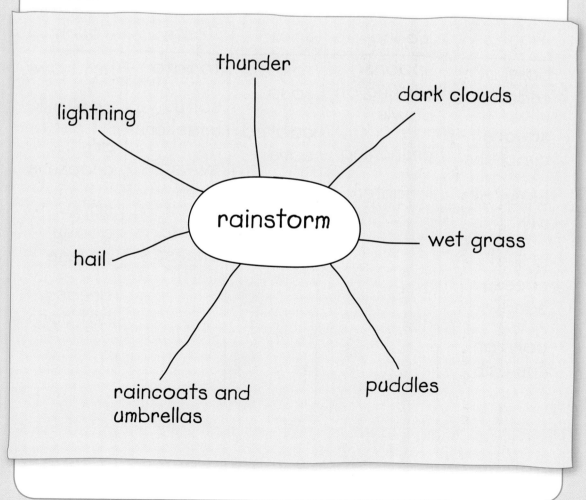

thunder

dark clouds

lightning

rainstorm

wet grass

hail

raincoats and umbrellas

puddles

Gather details with a sensory chart.

Use a **sensory chart** to list the sight, sound, smell, taste, and touch details for a topic.

Sensory Chart

Topic: Lunch

Sight	Sound	Smell	Taste	Touch
bowl of red soup	spoons clinking on bowls	tomato soup	tomato	hot bowl
square crackers	crunching	cooked corn	salty crackers	cool milk
glass of milk	laughter	toasted bread	sweet corn	dry crackers
grilled cheese sandwich			melted cheese	soft, gooey cheese
corn on the cob				greasy, hot corn

Plan a story with a map.

Use a **story map** to help you remember important parts of a story. You can draw pictures or write words to make a story map.

Story Map

Tortoise and the Hare

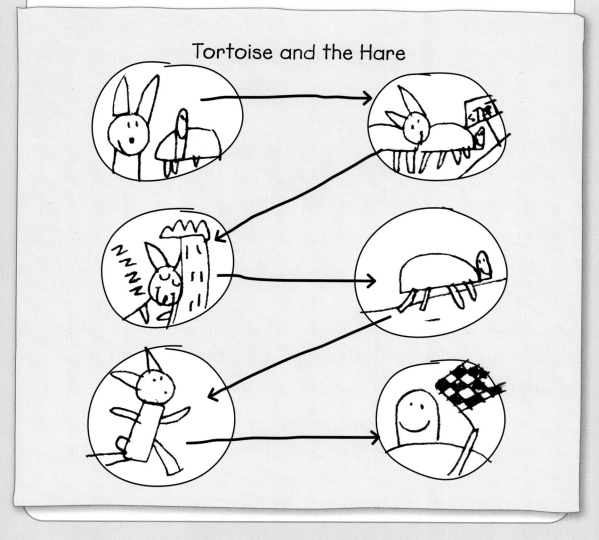

Gather facts with a 5 W's chart.

Make a **5 W's chart** when you need to find important facts or details for your writing.

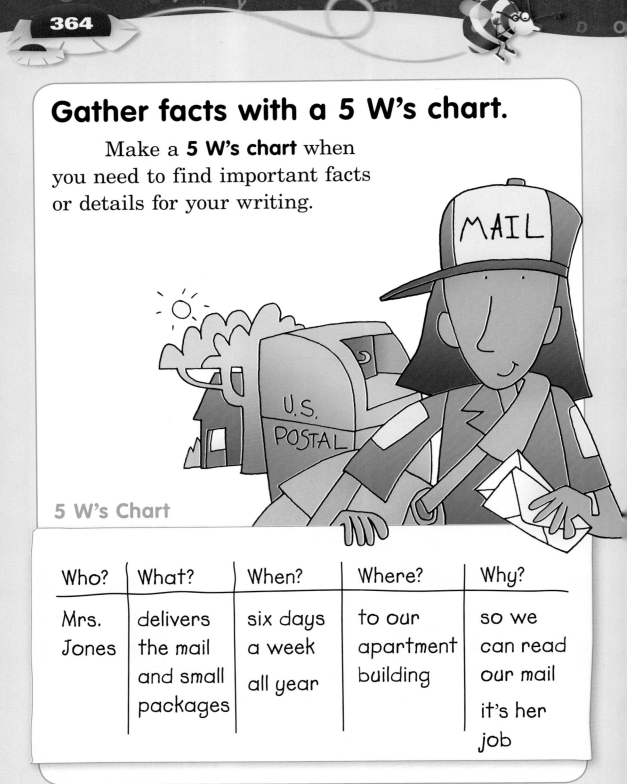

5 W's Chart

Who?	What?	When?	Where?	Why?
Mrs. Jones	delivers the mail and small packages	six days a week all year	to our apartment building	so we can read our mail it's her job

Put events in order with a time line.

Make a **time line** to show when different events happened. A time line can use hours, days, months, or years.

Sample Time Line

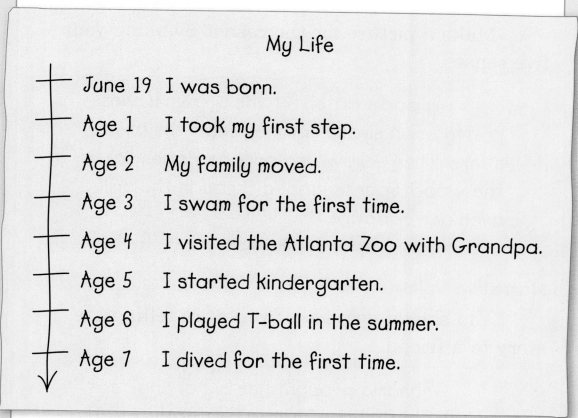

My Life

June 19   I was born.

Age 1   I took my first step.

Age 2   My family moved.

Age 3   I swam for the first time.

Age 4   I visited the Atlanta Zoo with Grandpa.

Age 5   I started kindergarten.

Age 6   I played T-ball in the summer.

Age 7   I dived for the first time.

How should my writing voice change?

Your voice should match your purpose.

Whenever you write, be yourself. Your writing voice should sound like you.

Descriptive Voice

Make a picture for the reader by using your five senses.

> My dad's match hit the brown leaves. Pretty soon smoke came up from the pile of sticks. Then yellow and orange flames licked the wood. Sparks jumped through the grill over our campfire.

Narrative Voice

You should write as if you were telling the story to a friend.

> Grandma brought her big orange cat to our house. Now I had a big job to do. I had to take care of Felix for two weeks. If you knew Felix, you would say, "Good luck!"

Expository Voice

You should know your topic and use specific details to explain it. Help your reader follow the steps.

> First, you spread glue where you want the glitter on your drawing. Next, sprinkle the glitter on the glue. Let it dry for a minute. Then shake the extra glitter off. Finally, let your picture dry completely.

Persuasive Voice

You should use good reasons to help the reader decide to agree with you.

> When you go outside on a very cold day, be sure to wear a hat. You lose a lot of heat from the top of your head. A hat helps to keep your whole body warm.

How can I learn new words?

Keep a new-word notebook.

Keep a notebook just for new words. Write each word and its meaning. Then write a sentence that uses the word. Add drawings if you wish.

New Word Notebook

Word	Meaning	Sentence	Drawing
telescope	an instrument used to look at stars	Mara's family bought a telescope to look at the moon.	
tanker	a truck or ship that carries liquids like water, milk, or oil	The tanker truck pulled out of the gas station.	

Use a dictionary.

You can learn what a word means by looking it up in a dictionary.

Sample Dictionary Entry

Sarah watches the red **insect** cross the sidewalk.

Insect An **insect** is a small animal with six legs. A wasp is a flying **insect**. Some common **insects** are crickets, moths, and mosquitoes.

Use a thesaurus.

A **thesaurus** is a book that lists words and their synonyms (words with the same meanings). Use a thesaurus to choose clear words.

Sample Thesaurus Entry

jacket *noun* coat, parka, windbreaker

General Word Choice
Larry wore a **jacket** to the football game.

Clear Word Choice
Larry wore a **parka** to the football game.

How else can I learn new words?

Use context clues.

Context clues are hints you find by reading the words all around a new word. These hints can help you figure out the meaning of the new word.

- Read the words after the new word.

> The **botanist** studied plants in the rain forest.

(The words *studied plants* give you a clue about the meaning of the word *botanist.*)

- Look for words with the same meaning.

> The **miniature** poodle looked very small.

(The words *very small* mean the same thing as the word *miniature.*)

- Study pictures that show what a word means.

> The cowboy **lassos** the calf.

COWBOYS

How can I learn word meanings?

Divide the word into parts.

You can figure out the meaning of a new word by learning about *prefixes, roots,* and *suffixes.*

Word: reviewer

Prefix: re   means "again"
Root: view means "to look at carefully"
Suffix: er   means "someone who does something"

A movie *reviewer* is someone who looks carefully again at a movie.

Learn prefixes.

A prefix is a word part that comes before the root. A prefix changes the meaning of the root word.

pre- (before)

pre**test** (before the final test)

re- (again)

re**build** (build something again)

un- (not)

un**clear** (not clear)

Learn suffixes.

A suffix is a word part that comes after a root word. A suffix changes the meaning of the root word.

-er, -or (a person who does something)

coal miner (a person who digs for coal)

-ful (full)

playful (full of play)

-ing (doing something)

walking (doing what it is to walk)

-less (not having something)

sugarless (having no sugar)

-ment (act of)

government (act of governing)

Remember root words.

The **root** is the main part of a word, without a prefix or a suffix. Study these roots.

cycl (wheel, circular)

> **bi**cyc**le** (a vehicle with two wheels)

fill (to make full)

> **re**fill (fill again)

flex (bend)

> flex**ible** (able to bend)

graph (write)

> **auto**graph (to write your own name)

mar (sea)

> **sub**mar**ine** (an undersea ship)

meter (measure)

> **thermo**meter (an instrument that measures temperature)

narr (tell)

> **narr**ative (writing that tells a story)

photo (light)

> **photo**graph (a picture formed by light)

port (carry)

> **trans**port**ation** (ways things are carried)

sphere (ball)

> **spher**ical (shaped like a ball)

teach (teach)

> **teach**er (a person who teaches)

tele (far)

> **tele**scope (an instrument for seeing things that are far away)

How can I connect my sentences?

Use time-order words.

Use **time-order words** to tell the order in which things happen or should be done.

Time-Order Word Chart

first	second	third
May 10	May 11	May 12
yesterday	today	tomorrow
then	now	later
first	next	last

Use place-order words.

Use **place-order words** to show location.

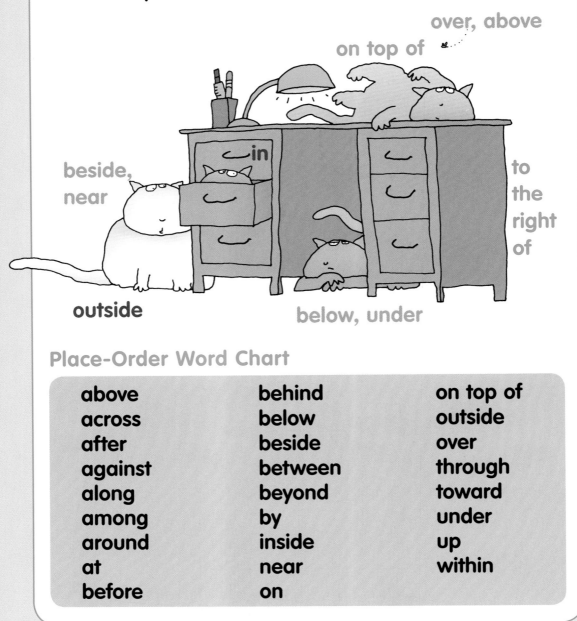

Place-Order Word Chart

above	behind	on top of
across	below	outside
after	beside	over
against	between	through
along	beyond	toward
among	by	under
around	inside	up
at	near	within
before	on	

How can I make my report better?

Add a bar graph.

A **bar graph** can help the reader understand numbers you use in your writing. The bars compare two or more things. The graph below shows the number of library books read in three different classrooms during one month.

Sample Bar Graph

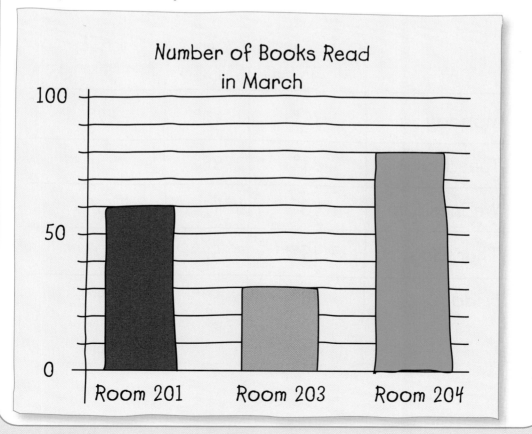

Add a chart.

A **chart** can help you collect and organize information. The chart below shows temperature changes for one week.

This Week's Temperatures

DAY	MORNING	NOON	LATE AFTERNOON
Monday	35°	40°	42°
Tuesday	33°	36°	36°
Wednesday	40°	47°	45°
Thursday	45°	52°	50°
Friday	46°	52°	54°

Draw a diagram.

A **diagram** is a picture that explains what something looks like or how it works. A diagram can help the reader understand your information better.

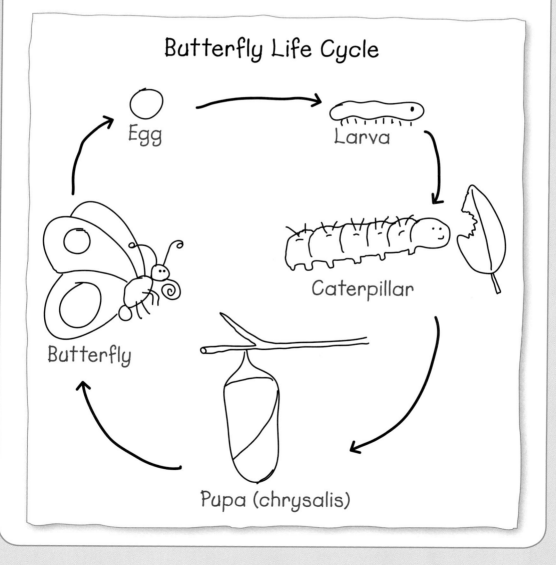

Butterfly Life Cycle

Egg

Larva

Caterpillar

Pupa (chrysalis)

Butterfly

Proofreader's Guide

Using Punctuation

A **walk** signal tells you to go. A **don't walk** signal tells you to stop. These signals are very important.

Stopping **and** Going

Punctuation marks are signals you use in writing. For example, you use a period to signal a stop at the end of a sentence. You use a comma to signal a pause. This chapter will tell you all about using punctuation.

Use a Period

At the End of a Telling Sentence

George and Martha are silly.

After an Initial

S. E. Goode

D. L. Spruce

Susan B. Anthony

After an Abbreviation

Mr. Plant

Ms. Blossom

Dr. Weed

Periods

Read the sentences below. Find where a period is missing. Write the word that comes before the missing period and then add the period.

Example: My teacher's name is
Ms Potter.
Ms.

1. Simon brings his lunch to school every day

2. His mother is Dr Brown.

3. She signs her name "Gina M Brown" on school forms.

4. Mr Brown is a carpenter.

5. Carpenters make things out of wood

6. Simon has a friend named T J Roberts.

Next Step: Write a sentence about your teacher. Include his or her name in your sentence.

Use a Question Mark

After a Question

Who sat on my lunch?

Use an Exclamation Point

After a Sentence That Shows Strong Feeling

Uh-oh, there's a skunk on the playground!

After a Word That Shows Excitement

Wow! Help!

Question Marks and Exclamation Points

Decide if each sentence below needs to end with a question mark or an exclamation point. Copy the sentences and end each with the correct punctuation mark.

Example: Hooray, the sun's coming out

Hooray, the sun's coming out!

1. Is the storm over

2. Wow, that storm was bad

3. The wind blew so hard

4. Did the wind blow anything over

5. Was there any flooding

6. Gosh, storms scare me

Next Step: Write two sentences about a bad storm. Make one sentence a question. Make the other sentence show strong feelings.

Use a Comma

A comma looks like a period with a tail on it (**,**).

Between Words in a Series

I love red **,** purple **,** and silver.

In Compound Sentences

Those colors are nice **,** but I like the color green best of all.

(In compound sentences, the comma is put in front of the conjuctions and, but, and so.)

To Help Set Off a Speaker's Words

Russ said **,** "I love kickball!"

Commas 1

■ Commas in a Series
■ Commas in Compound Sentences

For each sentence, write the word or words that should be followed by a comma. Write the comma, too.

Example: I see Canada Mexico and the United States on this globe.
Canada, Mexico,

1. Juan has family in Ohio Utah and Florida.

2. Some kids in my class have been to Ohio and Florida but none have visited Utah.

3. Ashley has cousins in Ohio Texas and Maine.

4. Her cousin from Maine asked her to visit so she went there last summer.

Next Step: Write a sentence about three places you'd like to visit someday.

Use a Comma

Between a City and a State
El Paso, Texas

Between the Day and the Year
January 28, 2006

After the Greeting and Closing in a Letter
Dear Grandpa,   Love,
                                 Liz

After Introductory Words
When we race, J. J. likes to win.

To Name a Person Spoken to
Annie, wait for me!

Commas 2

- ■ Commas in Dates and Addresses
- ■ Commas in Letter Writing

Copy the friendly letter. Add commas where they are needed.

Example: February 2 1998
February 2, 1998

254 Red Street
Lawton MI 49065
January 27 2006

Dear Groundhog

  Please cover your eyes when you come out of your burrow this year. I am tired of winter.

      Sincerely
      Bruce Limm

Next Step: Write a sentence using today's date.

Use an Apostrophe

To Make a Contraction

Two Words	Contraction
do not	don't
has not	hasn't
can not	can't
she is	she's
it is	it's
I am	I'm
we will	we'll
they will	they'll
is not	isn't
will not	won't
we are	we're
they are	they're

Apostrophes 1

■ Apostrophes to Make
Contractions

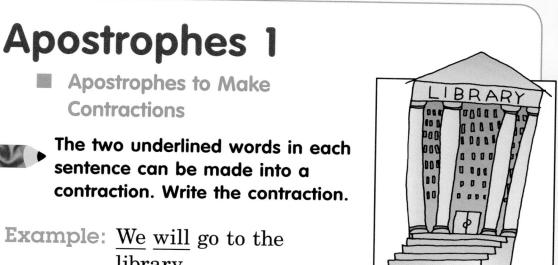

The two underlined words in each sentence can be made into a contraction. Write the contraction.

Example: We will go to the library.
We'll

1. We <u>do</u> <u>not</u> have to pay for books at the library.

2. <u>It</u> <u>is</u> a place where we can borrow them.

3. <u>I</u> <u>am</u> allowed to borrow books with my library card.

4. My sister Emma <u>can</u> <u>not</u> have her own library card.

5. <u>She</u> <u>is</u> just a baby!

Next Step: Use a contraction in a sentence about your school library.

Use an Apostrophe

To Show Ownership

This is Mary's book

The tree's leaves are falling.

Harold is my brother's frog.
(One brother owns the frog.)

My brothers' frogs jump high.
(Each brother owns a frog.)

Apostrophes 2

■ **Apostrophes to Show Ownership**

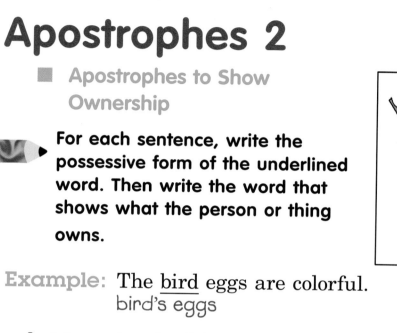

For each sentence, write the possessive form of the underlined word. Then write the word that shows what the person or thing owns.

Example: The <u>bird</u> eggs are colorful.
bird's eggs

1. <u>Mom</u> ring is shiny.

2. I want to read <u>Mr. Green</u> book.

3. We found the <u>girl</u> backpack.

4. Do you know where <u>Becky</u> glasses are?

5. The <u>van</u> tire is flat.

Next Step: Write a sentence about something that belongs to your teacher. Use an apostrophe to show ownership.

Use Underlining

For Titles of Books and Magazines

I read <u>The Mouse That Snored.</u>

<u>Ranger Rick</u> comes in the mail.

Use Quotation Marks

Before and After a Speaker's Words

"I love carrots," said Sam.

Underlining and Quotation Marks

Copy each sentence. Put quotation marks around a speaker's words. Underline any titles.

Example: Hi, Jared, said my dad.
"Hi, Jared," said my dad.

1. When are you coming home? I asked.

2. He said, Soon. I have a surprise for you.

3. My dad brought me a book called Lisa's Airplane Trip.

4. Thanks, Dad, I said.

Next Step: Write a sentence that tells the title of a book.

Practice Test

Read each sentence. A punctuation mark is needed in each box. Write the letter that shows the correct mark.

1. Are these flowers real ☐
   a. . *(period)*   **b.** ? *(question mark)*

2. Martha said, ☐ I like bananas."
   a. " *(quotation mark)*   **b.** ' *(apostrophe)*

3. Our scout leader is Ms ☐ Cannon.
   a. . *(period)*   **b.** ' *(apostrophe)*

4. I didn ☐ t bring my boots today.
   a. " *(quotation mark)*   **b.** ' *(apostrophe)*

5. We saw lions ☐ monkeys, and bears at the zoo.
   a. , *(comma)*   **b.** ' *(apostrophe)*

6. I found Jacob ☐ s shoe behind the chair.
   a. , *(comma)*   **b.** ' *(apostrophe)*

7. Lena was born on January 14 ☐ 1999.
   a. , *(comma)*   **b.** ' *(apostrophe)*

Checking
Mechanics

Rules help you in many ways. There are rules for keeping you safe. There are rules for playing games. There are also rules for writing.

Rules for Writing

This chapter lists many rules for the **mechanics of writing**. You will learn about using capital letters, writing plurals, and much more. Following these rules helps your reader to understand what you write.

Use Capital Letters

For All Proper Nouns

Names, Titles, and Initials

Jackie Wilson

Dr. Small

E. B. White

For Days, Months, and Holidays

Friday   January   Thanksgiving

For Names of Places

Canada	Rocky Mountains
Ohio	Main Street
Chicago	Sears Tower

Capitalization 1

■ Proper Nouns

Write all the words that should be capitalized in the sentences below. The number in ( ) tells how many words you should find in each sentence.

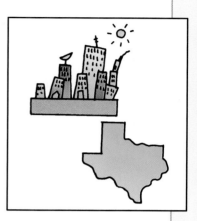

Example: We live on oak road
in vicksburg. (3)
Oak Road, Vicksburg

1. Mom and I wanted to surprise Dad for father's day. (2)

2. We asked Dad's old friend to meet us on sunday, june 14, in austin, texas. (4)

3. Dad and mr. hanks grew up in austin. (3)

4. Now Dad lives in dallas, and mr. hanks lives in houston. (4)

Next Step: Write a sentence that tells the name of the place you live.

Use Capital Letters

For the First Word in a Sentence

Fireflies light up the garden.

For a Speaker's First Word

Mr. Smith said, "Look at this spiderweb."

For the Word "I"

What will I say to him?

For Titles of Books, Stories, Poems, . . .

Aesop's Fox (book)

"Lost in the Woods" (story)

"Elephant for Sale" (poem)

Spider (magazine)

Capitalization 2

■ First Words
■ The Word "I"
■ Titles

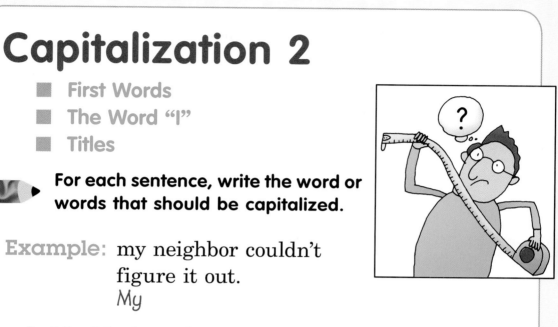

► For each sentence, write the word or words that should be capitalized.

Example: my neighbor couldn't figure it out.
My

1. Mr. Mark said, "this shelf should fit right here!"

2. he measured the space again.

3. then he looked in a book called *wood works.*

4. Mr. Mark also looked at a magazine article called "building shelves."

5. he looked at the pictures.

6. He said, "i made a mistake!"

Next Step: What do you think Mr. Mark did wrong? Write a sentence telling about it.

Make Plurals

Add -s to make the plural of most nouns.

boy → boy**s**   wing → wing**s**

shoe → shoe**s**   book → book**s**

Add -es to make the plural of nouns ending in *s*, *x*, *sh*, *ch*, and *z*.

glass → glass**es**   inch → inch**es**

fox → fox**es**   buzz → buzz**es**

bush → bush**es**

Plurals 1

- Most Nouns
- Nouns Ending in *ch, s, sh,* and *x*

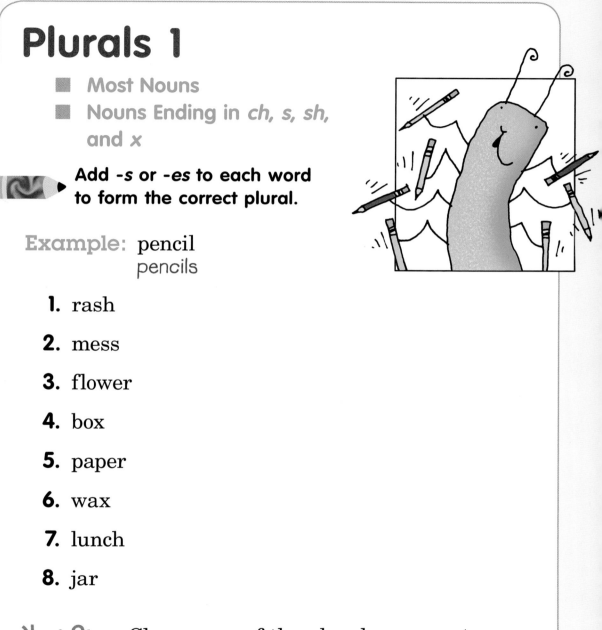

Add *-s* or *-es* to each word to form the correct plural.

Example: pencil
pencils

1. rash

2. mess

3. flower

4. box

5. paper

6. wax

7. lunch

8. jar

Next Step: Choose one of the plurals you wrote. Write a sentence using the word.

Make Plurals

Change the word to make the plural of some nouns. These are called "irregular" plurals.

child ➔ **children**   man ➔ **men**

foot ➔ **feet**   goose ➔ **geese**

Change the _y_ to _i_ and add _-es_ to nouns that end with a consonant plus a _y_.

sky ➔ sk**ies**   story ➔ stor**ies**

ferry ➔ ferr**ies**   baby ➔ bab**ies**

Plurals 2

- ■ Nouns Ending in a Consonant + y
- ■ Irregular Plurals

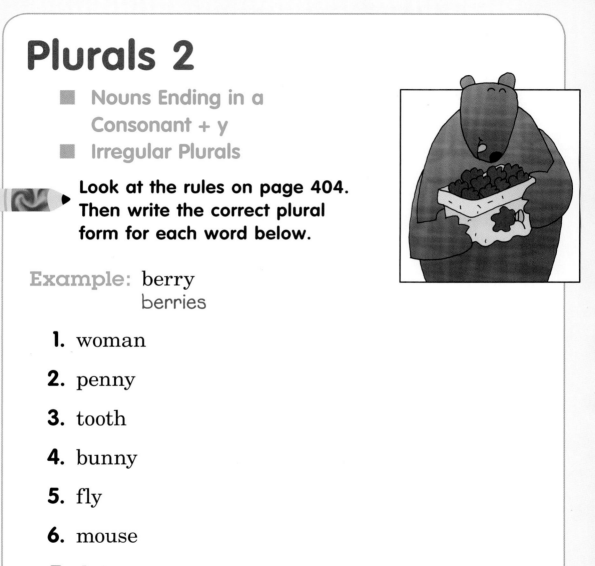

Look at the rules on page 404. Then write the correct plural form for each word below.

Example: berry
berries

1. woman

2. penny

3. tooth

4. bunny

5. fly

6. mouse

7. daisy

8. man

Next Step: Choose one of the plural words you wrote. Write a sentence using that word.

Use Abbreviations

For Titles of People

Mister → **Mr.**   Doctor → **Dr.**

For Days of the Week

Sunday	Sun.	Thursday	Thurs.
Monday	Mon.	Friday	Fri.
Tuesday	Tues.	Saturday	Sat.
Wednesday	Wed.		

For Months of the Year

January	Jan.	July	July
February	Feb.	August	Aug.
March	Mar.	September	Sept.
April	Apr.	October	Oct.
May	May	November	Nov.
June	June	December	Dec.

Post Office Address Abbreviations

Avenue	AVE	Road	RD
Drive	DR	South	S
East	E	Street	ST
North	N	West	W

Abbreviations

▶ **Write the abbreviation for each underlined word.**

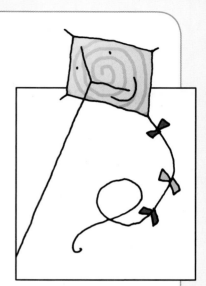

Example: <u>March</u> winds
Mar.

1. 123 Oak <u>Avenue</u>

2. Friday, <u>August</u> 29

3. 555 State <u>Road</u>

4. <u>January</u> 3

5. 869 <u>South</u> Main Street

6. Thursday, <u>September</u> 18

Next Step: Write the correct abbreviations for all
the days of the week.

Practice Test

Read the paragraphs below. For each underlined part, choose the letter of the best way to write it.

          1
<u>Next friday</u> my cousin is having a party.

We will have popcorn and fruit juice. We will
                 2
play games. All <u>my cousin</u> will be there.

1. **a.** next Friday
    b. Next Friday
    c. correct as is

2. **a.** my cousins
    b. my Cousins
    c. correct as is

                        3
Debby's dog has six new <u>puppys</u>. They are
      4
so cute! <u>I wish</u> one could be mine!

3. **a.** puppyes
    b. puppies
    c. correct as is

4. **a.** i wish
    b. I Wish
    c. correct as is

Checking
Your Spelling

The spelling list that follows on pages 410-416 is in ABC order. It includes many of the important words you will use in your writing. Check this list when you are not sure how to spell a word. (Also check a classroom dictionary for help.)

Use a SPELLING PLAN

- Look at the word and say it.
- Spell it aloud.
- Say the word again, sound by sound.
- Notice the spelling of each sound.
- Cover the word and write it on paper.
- Check the spelling.
- If you make a mistake, try again.

A

about
after
again
all
alone
and
animal
another
are
as
ask
aunt
away

B

back
bad
bank
be
because
been

before
bell
best
big
black
blue
boat
book
born
both
box
bright
bring
broke
brother
brown
burn
but
by

C

call
candle
card
children
clean
clock
color
come
could
cousin
crowd

D

daddy
dance
dark
dear
didn't
doesn't
dogs
doll
dollars
done
don't
door
dream
drop

Spelling 1

Look at the picture in front of each phrase below. Write a word from your spelling list to fill in the blank.

Example: 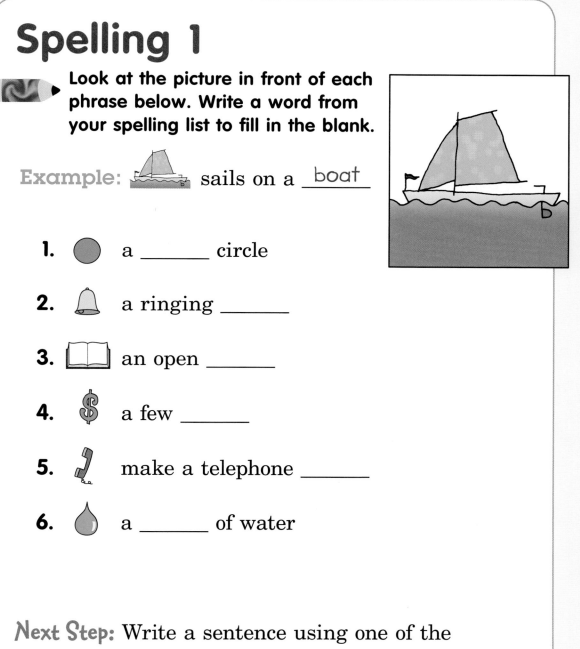 sails on a ___boat___

1. ● a _____ circle

2. 🔔 a ringing _____

3. 📖 an open _____

4. $ a few _____

5. ☎ make a telephone _____

6. 💧 a _____ of water

Next Step: Write a sentence using one of the phrases above.

E

each
eat
eight
end
eye

F

fall
far
fast
feather
feel
fight
fire
first
five
floor
flowers
fly
food
foot
for

forgot
found
four
Friday
friend
from
front
full
fun
funny

G

game
girl
give
going
good
grandfather
grandmother
grass
green

H

had
hair
half
hand
happen
hard
has
have
head
help
her
here
hide
high
hill
his
home
hope
horse
hot
hour
how
hurt

I

I
ice
if
I'm
is
it's
I've

J

jam
jelly
just

K

keep
kids
kind
kitten
knew

Spelling 2

▶ **Write the correct word from your spelling list to fill in the blank in each sentence below.**

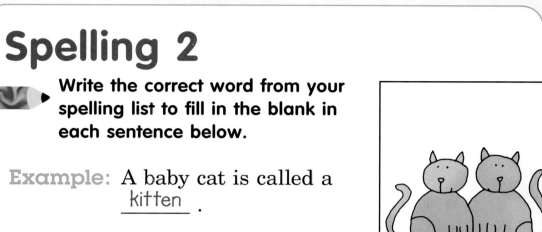

Example: A baby cat is called a
<u>kitten</u> .

1. The day after Thursday is
_____ .

2. A joke is a _____ story.

3. Frozen water is _____.

4. There are 60 minutes in an _____ .

5. I raise my _____ when I want to speak in class.

Next Step: Write a sentence using another word from your spelling list.

L

lady
land
last
laugh
leave
left
letter
light
live
long
look
lot
loud
love

M

made
make
many
may
men
milk

Monday
money
monkey
month
moon
more
morning
most
mother
move
much
must
my

N

name
need
new
next
nice
night
nine
not
now

O

of
off
okay
old
once
one
open
or
orange
other
our
out

P

party
pencil
penny
play
please
poor
porch
post

pour
pretty
pull
purple

Q

quick
quiet
quit

R

rabbit
rain
read
ready
really
ride
right
road
rode
room
rope

Spelling 3

Write a word from your spelling list to fill in the blank in each sentence below. Pay attention to the hints.

Example: A <u>r</u> <u>a</u> <u>b</u> <u>b</u> <u>i</u> <u>t</u> has long ears.

1. The sun does not shine at
   <u>n</u> __ __ <u>h</u> __ .

2. It rises every <u>m</u> __ __ <u>n</u> __ __ __ .

3. You may have an apple if you say
   <u>p</u> <u>l</u> __ __ __ __ .

4. Kris ate a juicy <u>o</u> __ __ __ __ __ .

5. My favorite color is <u>p</u> __ __ <u>p</u> __ __ .

Next Step: Write a sentence using another word from your spelling list.

S

said
Saturday
saw
say
says
school
seven
shoes
should
sister
six
sleep
soft
something
soon
sound
still
store
storm
street
summer
Sunday
sure

T

take
talk
teacher
teeth
tell
ten
thank
that
them
these
they
think
this
those
three
Thursday
told
tooth
try
Tuesday
two

U

uncle
under
until
use

V

van
very

W

walk
want
way
Wednesday
week
went
were
what
when
where
which

why
with
won
word
work
would
write

X

X-ray

Y

year
yellow
you
your
you're

Z

zipper
zoo

Spelling 4

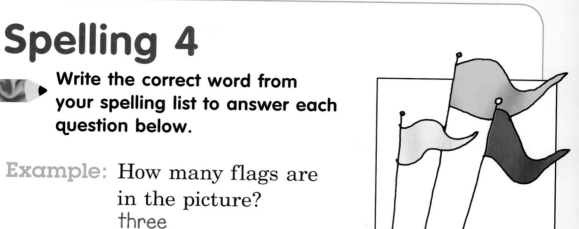

Write the correct word from your spelling list to answer each question below.

Example: How many flags are in the picture?
three

1. How many days are in a week?

2. Where do you go to see lions, monkeys, and bears?

3. What are the hard white things in your mouth?

4. What day comes after Tuesday?

5. What season is the hottest?

Next Step: Write a sentence using another word from your spelling list.

Practice Test

Read each sentence below. Then write the letter of the correct answer.

1. My older _____ plays games with me.
   a. bruther   **c.** brother
   b. bother   **d.** brothre

2. Earth's _____ comes from the sun.
   a. lite   **c.** ligth
   b. light   **d.** leit

3. We split the apple in _____ .
   a. half   **c.** haf
   b. halve   **d.** hafe

4. _____ is making a funny noise on the roof.
   a. Sumthing   **c.** Somthing
   c. Someting   **d.** Something

Using the
Right Word

Some words sound alike, but they have different spellings. They also have different meanings. These words are called **homophones**.

ant   Mom bought me an ant farm.

aunt   My aunt is my dad's sister.

ate   I ate a banana this morning.

eight   Shannon is eight years old.

bare   Look at my bare feet!

bear   The grizzly bear growled.

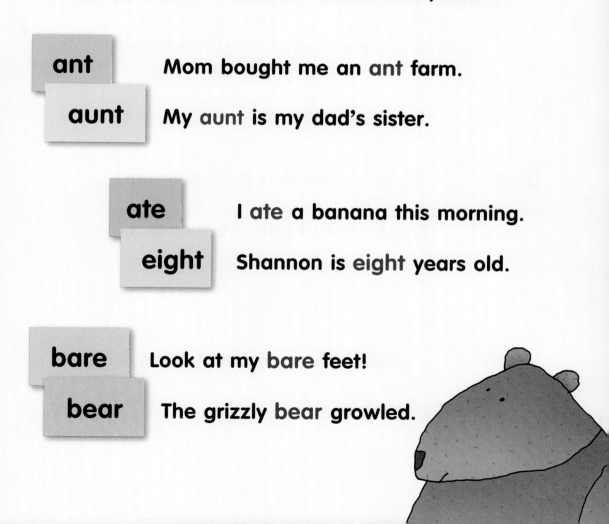

blew — Dakota **blew** the biggest bubble.

blue — A robin's egg is **blue**.

by — Place the spoon **by** the knife.

buy — We must **buy** some milk today.

dear — My grandma is a **dear** woman.

deer — The **deer** ran into the woods.

for — Miss Nelson made cookies **for** us.

four — Nick ate **four** tacos.

Using the Right Word 1

- blew, blue
- buy, by
- dear, deer
- for, four

For each sentence, write the correct word from the choice given.

Example: Jimmy *(blew, blue)* into the whistle toy.
blew

1. It was his *(dear, deer)* grandma's birthday!

2. She told Jim not to *(buy, by)* a gift.

3. He made a painting *(for, four)* her.

4. He used a lot of *(blew, blue)* paint.

5. He painted a *(dear, deer)* with antlers.

6. He painted *(for, four)* kinds of flowers, too.

Next Step: Write a sentence telling about a picture you would like to paint. Use the word *by* in your sentence.

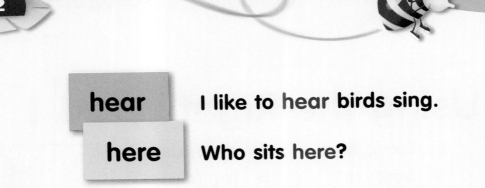

hear   I like to hear birds sing.

here   Who sits here?

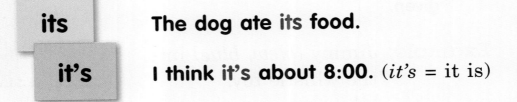

its   The dog ate its food.

it's   I think it's about 8:00. (*it's* = it is)

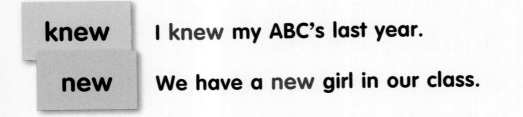

knew   I knew my ABC's last year.

new   We have a new girl in our class.

know   Do you know her name?

no   Robert said, "No, I don't."

Using the Right Word 2

- hear, here
- knew, new
- its, it's
- know, no

Write the correct word for each sentence.

Example: I have a *(knew, new)* joke to tell you.

new

1. Maxine, are you ready to *(hear, here)* it?

2. *(Its, It's)* about bees going to school.

3. Do you *(know, no)* how they get there?

4. Maxine said, "*(Know, No)*, tell me."

5. A bee gets to school on *(its, it's)* buzz.

6. She laughed and said, "I *(knew, new)* it would be a funny one!"

Next Step: Write a sentence telling how *you* get to school. Use one of the blue words at the top of the page in your sentence.

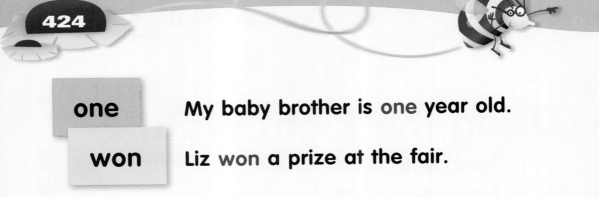

one   My baby brother is **one** year old.

won   Liz **won** a prize at the fair.

their   We used **their** bikes.
                (*Their* shows ownership.)

there   **There** are four of them.

they're   **They're** mountain bikes.
                (*they're* = they are)

to   I like **to** read funny books.

two   I read **two** joke books today.

too   Joe likes joke books, **too**.

Using the Right Word 3

- one, won
- their, there, they're
- to, two, too

▶ **Write the correct word for each sentence.**

Example: Mom *(one, won)* a fruit basket as a prize at the school carnival.
won

1. The basket had *(one, won)* apple in it.

2. It had bananas, *(to, too, two)*.

3. *(Their, There, They're)* were some cherries, too.

4. Mom is going *(to, too, two)* make a fruit salad.

5. Dad will eat *(to, too, two)* bowls of fruit.

Next Step: Write a sentence about winning a prize. Use the word *their* in your sentence.

Antonyms

Antonyms are two words with opposite meanings. Here are some common antonyms you should know.

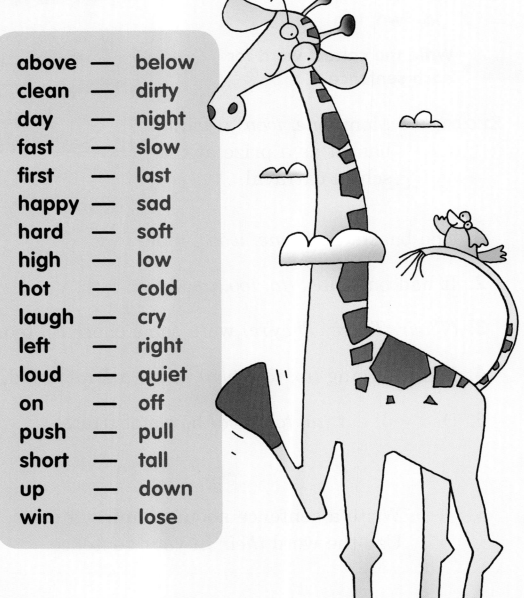

above	—	below
clean	—	dirty
day	—	night
fast	—	slow
first	—	last
happy	—	sad
hard	—	soft
high	—	low
hot	—	cold
laugh	—	cry
left	—	right
loud	—	quiet
on	—	off
push	—	pull
short	—	tall
up	—	down
win	—	lose

Antonyms

Finish each sentence below with the opposite (antonym) of the word under the line.

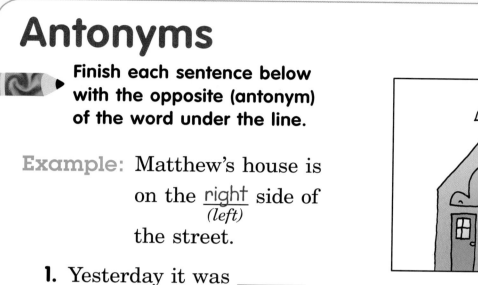

Example: Matthew's house is on the <u>right</u> side of
(left)
the street.

1. Yesterday it was _____ outside.
(cold)

2. The teacher asked the children to be

_____.
(loud)

3. It's too bad we did not _____ this game.
(lose)

4. Someone left the light _____.
(off)

5. I like my pillow. It is not too _____.
(hard)

Next Step: Write a sentence like those above. Use any pair of antonyms that was not used here.

Practice Test

Choose the right word to complete each sentence.
Write the letter "a" or "b" on your paper.

1. The bear took our food in _____ mouth.
  a. its   **b.** it's

2. The antonym for *on* is _____ .
  a. of   **b.** off

3. The Bitville Tigers _____ the game.
  a. won   **b.** one

4. We'll have our picnic _____ at the park.
  a. hear   **b.** here

5. It is too wet on the ground over _____ .
  a. their   **b.** there

6. The antonym for *down* is _____ .
  a. up   **b.** across

Understanding
Sentences

A **sentence** tells a complete idea and has two parts.

1. The subject is the naming part.

2. The predicate (verb) is the telling part.

The verb tells what the subject is doing.

My <u>mom</u> <u>rides</u> a motorcycle.

   subject   verb

A **sentence** begins with a capital letter. It ends with a period, a question mark, or an exclamation point.

Grandpa climbs trees.

Can he reach the top?

Wow, he is way up there!

The Subject

The **subject** is the naming part of a sentence. It tells you who or what the sentence is about. A subject is usually a noun that names a person, place, or thing.

> My new baby **sister** sleeps a lot.
> (*Sister* is the naming word in the subject.)

> **My new baby sister** sleeps a lot.
> (*My new baby sister* are all the words in the subject.)

> **The subject can also be a pronoun.**
> **She** went to the mall.
> **It** is a new car.
> **We** will listen to music.

Subject of a Sentence

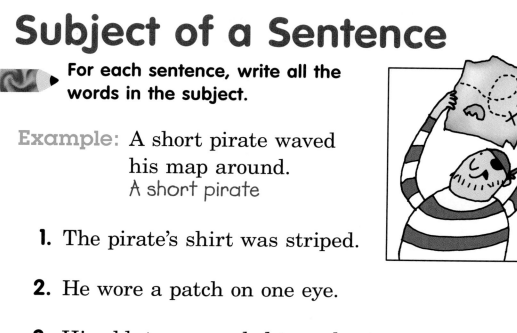

For each sentence, write all the words in the subject.

Example: A short pirate waved his map around.
A short pirate

1. The pirate's shirt was striped.

2. He wore a patch on one eye.

3. His old, torn map led to a chest.

4. A dotted line showed the way.

5. The chest could hold gold.

6. It could hold a very old book or a vase.

Next Step: Write a sentence about what kind of buried treasure the pirate found. Underline all the words in the subject.

The Predicate

The **predicate** of a sentence has the verb in it. It tells something about the subject or what the subject is doing.

My uncle Benny **builds** doghouses.
(*Builds* is the verb in the predicate.)

My uncle Benny **builds doghouses**.
(*Builds doghouses* are all the words in the predicate.)

That flower **is beautiful**.
(The predicate *is beautiful* tells something about the subject.)

Predicate of a Sentence

For each sentence, write all the words in the predicate.

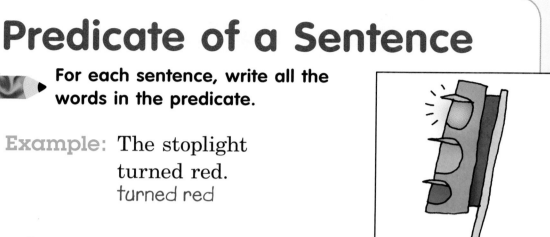

Example: The stoplight turned red.
turned red

1. Mom stopped the car.

2. Two kids pressed the *walk* button.

3. They crossed the street.

4. They were very careful.

5. The light changed to green.

6. They went on their way.

Next Step: Write a sentence about a car trip. Underline all the words in the predicate.

Kinds of Sentences

A **telling sentence** makes a statement.

Soccer is my favorite game.

An **asking sentence** asks a question.

Will you play with me?

A **command sentence** makes a request or gives directions.

Kick with the side of your foot.

An **exclamatory sentence** shows surprise or strong feelings.

Watch out for the ball!

Kinds of Sentences

**Write *T* for a telling sentence.
Write *A* for an asking sentence.
Write *E* for an exclamatory
sentence. Write *C* for a
command sentence.**

Example: How do birds stay dry
when it rains?
A

1. Feathers protect a bird from getting too wet.

2. Wow, some birds cannot fly!

3. Do you have a pet bird at home?

4. Clean its cage often.

5. My aunt has a myna bird.

6. Can a myna "talk" better than a parrot?

Next Step: Write a sentence about a bird. Ask
a classmate to tell what kind of
sentence you have written.

Practice Test

Read the sentences below. Look at the part of the sentence that is underlined. Write the letter that names the underlined part.

1. John <u>plays the piano</u>.
    a. subject   **b.** predicate

2. <u>Our music teacher</u> is the best!
    a. subject   **b.** predicate

Read each sentence. Write the letter that tells what kind of sentence it is.

3. Watch out for the bees!
    a. telling sentence   **b.** exclamatory sentence

4. Kerry plays soccer on Saturdays.
    a. telling sentence   **b.** command sentence

5. Do you like swimming lessons?
    a. exclamatory sentence   **b.** asking sentence

6. Tara, close the door.
    a. asking sentence   **b.** command sentence

Using the
Parts of Speech

All of the words you use fit into eight groups. These groups are called the **parts of speech**.

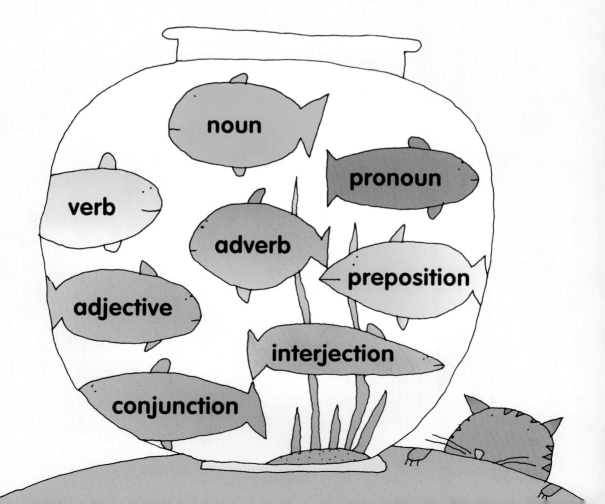

Nouns

A **noun** is a word that names a person, place, or thing.

person:	girl	firefighter
place:	house	school
thing:	bike	flower

Nouns can be **common** or **proper**.

common:	boy	street
proper:	Gus	Oak Street

Nouns 1

■ Common and Proper Nouns

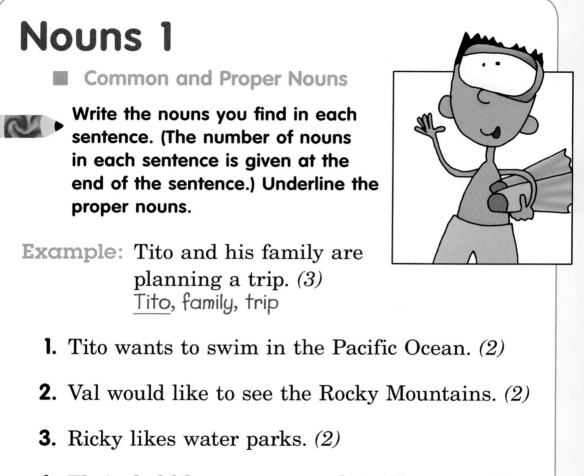

Write the nouns you find in each sentence. (The number of nouns in each sentence is given at the end of the sentence.) Underline the proper nouns.

Example: Tito and his family are
planning a trip. *(3)*
<u>Tito</u>, family, trip

1. Tito wants to swim in the Pacific Ocean. *(2)*

2. Val would like to see the Rocky Mountains. *(2)*

3. Ricky likes water parks. *(2)*

4. Their dad likes campgrounds in Vermont. *(3)*

5. Mrs. Rodriguez wants to rest at the beach. *(2)*

Next Step: Write a sentence about a trip you
would like to take. Ask a classmate to
underline each noun in your sentence.

Nouns

Nouns can be **singular** or **plural**.
singular: neighbor   house
plural: neighbors   houses

A **possessive noun** shows ownership.
Add **'s** after a singular noun.

    Julie's flute

    the **bird's** wings

Add only an apostrophe (**'**) after most plural nouns.

    The **boys'** camp is near the lake.

    There were eggs in both **birds'** nests.

Nouns 2

■ Singular and Plural Nouns
■ Possessive Nouns

Make two columns. Write the singular nouns from the paragraph below in one column. Write the plural nouns in the other column.

Example: Pamela watered the plants.

Singular	Plural
Pamela	plants

   Hank likes Mr. Green's garden. Mr. Green asked Hank and Pamela to help him. They dug a little hole for each seed. They planted tomatoes and potatoes. They also planted beans, peas, carrots, and onions. When they harvest their crops, they will have a big meal at Hasheem's house.

Next Step: Read the paragraph again. Write down two possessive nouns that you find.

Pronouns

A **pronoun** is a word that takes the place of a noun. Here are some pronouns.

singular:

I	my	your	her	him	it
me	you	she	he	his	its

plural:

we	you	our	them
us	your	they	their

Pronouns stand for nouns in sentences.

Holly played a game.

She hid the penny.

(*She* stands for *Holly*.)

Erik made a kite.

Then **he** flew **it**.

(*He* stands for *Erik*.

It stands for *kite*.)

Pronouns

For each sentence below, write the pronoun. Then write the noun it stands for.

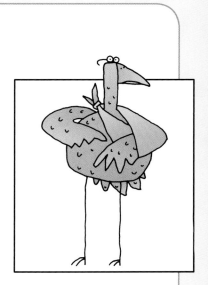

Example: The bird broke its wing.
  its – bird

1. Rena braids her long hair.

2. Davon, you may have a snack.

3. Mom made dinner, and the family enjoyed it.

4. Ted said, "That's my backpack."

5. Luke and Kenny raised their hands at the same time.

6. The teacher saw Luke first and picked him.

Next Step: Write one or two sentences about a friend. Use a pronoun to take the place of a noun.

Verbs

A **verb** is a word that shows action or helps complete a thought (linking verb).

Spot **barks** at my neighbor. (action verb)

Mr. Wilson **is** so mad! (linking verb)

Common Linking Verbs:

is	are	was	been
were	am	be	

Some Action Verbs:

ask	fix	jump	play
cook	help	listen	ride
dance	hug	move	stop

Verbs 1

■ **Action and Linking Verbs**

Write the verb in each sentence below. Then write *A* for action or *L* for linking.

Example: Katy listens to her CD.
listens, A

1. She owns a CD player.

2. Katy likes country music.

3. Her favorite song is "Country Mile."

4. Sometimes she dances to the music.

5. She is a good dancer.

6. Katy also sings well.

Next Step: Write one or two sentences about the kind of music you like. Underline the verb or verbs.

Verb Tenses

Some verbs tell what is happening now, or in the **present**.

Sarah **walks** her dog every morning.

Some verbs tell what happened in the **past**.

Sarah **walked** her dog last night.

(Many verbs in our language are **regular**. This means you add *-ed* to form the past tense.)

Some verbs tell what will happen in the **future**.

Sarah **will walk** her dog tomorrow.

Verbs 2

■ Verb Tenses

▶ **Write the action verb in each sentence below. Then write** *present, past,* **or** *future.*

Example: I save money in my
piggy bank.
save, present

1. Tina saved more than six dollars last month.

2. She puts all her change in a pretty box.

3. Jane will buy a new baseball glove.

4. Her brother gave his old glove to Jane.

5. She wants a catcher's mitt.

6. The baseball season will start in a few weeks.

Next Step: Write a sentence about saving money.
What verb tense did you use?

Irregular Verbs

Some verbs are **irregular**. You usually can't add -ed to them. They change in different ways.

Present Tense	Past Tense	With Helping Verb
am, is, are	was, were	been
begin	began	begun
break	broke	broken
catch	caught	caught
come	came	come
draw	drew	drawn
eat	ate	eaten
fall	fell	fallen
give	gave	given
go	went	gone
hide	hid	hidden, hid
know	knew	known
ride	rode	ridden
run	ran	run
see	saw	seen
sing	sang, sung	sung
take	took	taken
throw	threw	thrown
write	wrote	written

Verbs 3

■ **Irregular Verbs**

Read each sentence below. Complete each with the past tense of the verb in parentheses. (Look on page 448 for help.)

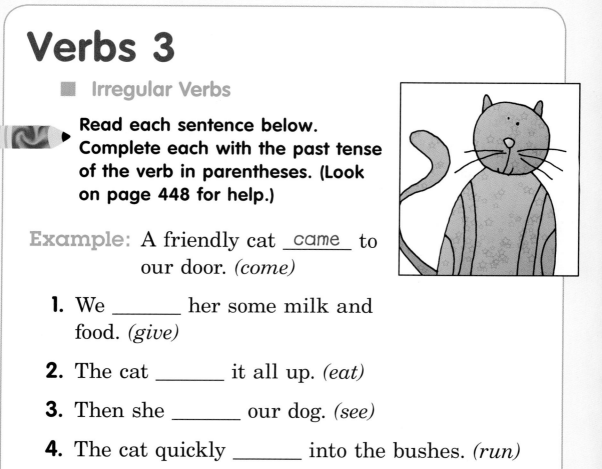

Example: A friendly cat <u>came</u> to our door. *(come)*

1. We _____ her some milk and food. *(give)*

2. The cat _____ it all up. *(eat)*

3. Then she _____ our dog. *(see)*

4. The cat quickly _____ into the bushes. *(run)*

5. She _____ there for a long time. *(hide)*

Next Step: Write a sentence about an animal. Use the past tense form of an irregular verb.

Adjectives

An **adjective** is a word that describes a noun or pronoun.

> **Large** snakes live in the jungle.
>
> An anaconda is a **giant** one!

The words *a, an,* and *the* are **articles**.
Use *a* before a consonant sound:

> **a** parrot

Use *an* before a vowel sound:

> **an** otter

Adjectives 1

■ Adjectives and Articles

Write the adjectives and articles from each sentence below. The number in ( ) tells you how many you will find.

Example: The old airplane flew in circles. *(2)*
The, old

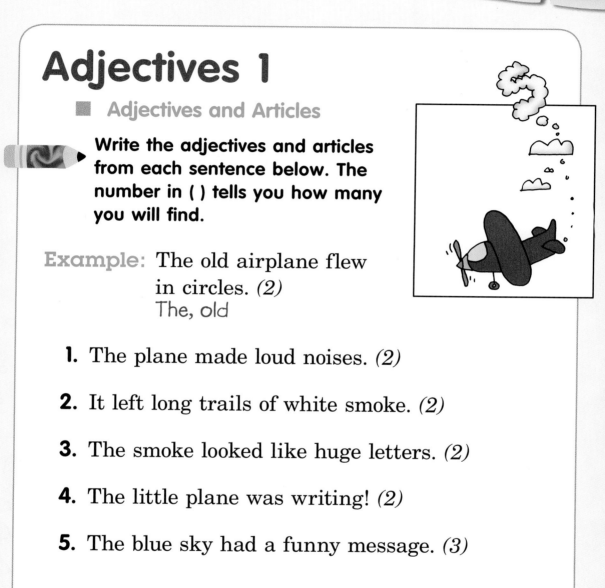

1. The plane made loud noises. *(2)*

2. It left long trails of white smoke. *(2)*

3. The smoke looked like huge letters. *(2)*

4. The little plane was writing! *(2)*

5. The blue sky had a funny message. *(3)*

Next Step: Write a sentence that tells what the plane wrote. Use adjectives and articles.

Adjectives That Compare

An **adjective** sometimes compares two nouns (or pronouns).

> An ant is **smaller** than an anaconda.
>
> A lion's roar is **louder** than a cat's meow.

An **adjective** can also compare more than two nouns.

> An anteater is the **oddest** animal.
>
> The **biggest** mammal in the world is the whale.

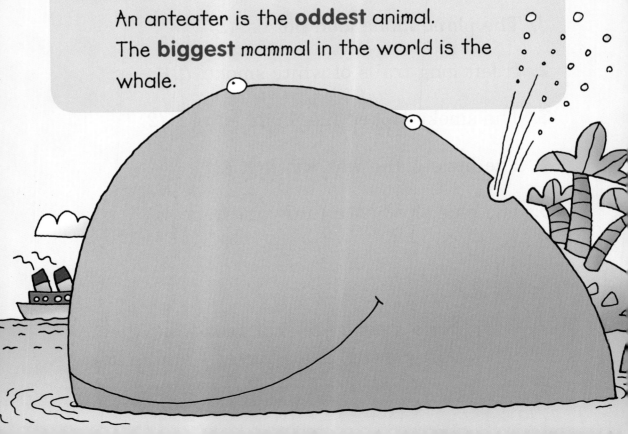

Adjectives 2

■ Adjectives That Compare

For each sentence, write the correct adjective.

Example: An elephant is *(bigger, biggest)* than a hippo.
bigger

1. The *(hotter, hottest)* place in the United States is Death Valley.

2. A cheetah is the *(faster, fastest)* animal on land.

3. The Nile River is *(longer, longest)* than the Ohio River.

4. Jill has the *(darker, darkest)* hair of anyone in our class.

5. My dog is *(smaller, smallest)* than Ken's dog.

Next Step: Write a sentence that includes an adjective that compares.

Adverbs

An **adverb** is a word that describes a verb.
It can tell *how, where,* or *when.*

How:	Erin ran **quickly**.
Where:	She fell **down**.
When:	She has fallen **before**.

Here are some other adverbs.

How:	brightly	carefully	easily
	fast	loudly	quietly
Where:	away	forward	nearby
	outside	there	upstairs
When:	always	first	often
	weekly	yearly	yesterday

Adverbs

Write the adverb you find in each sentence below. Hint: Look for the action verb first.

Example: The fish swam away.
away

1. Teddy quietly read his book.

2. We went swimming yesterday.

3. Mom slowly added milk to the gravy.

4. Sunflowers grow fast.

5. Donna walks there.

6. The airplane glided smoothly to a stop.

Next Step: Write a sentence that uses an adverb.

Prepositions, Conjunctions, and Interjections

A **preposition** is used to help make a statement.

Maya laughed **at** the joke.

Joe sat **on** the beach.

A **conjunction** connects words or ideas.

I will dance **or** sing.

First I cried, **and** then I laughed.

An **interjection** shows excitement.

Wow! Did you see that bug?

Yuck! I hate creepy crawlers!

Prepositions, Interjections, and Conjunctions

 ▶ **Write the correct word to complete each sentence.**

Example: *(Wow, Oh no)*, Isabel is a good cheerleader!
Wow

Prepositions

1. Jake ran *(up, in)* the stairs.

2. We can walk *(at, to)* the store.

Conjunctions

3. I can choose a pear *(or, but)* an apple.

4. Ned's family has a cat *(so, and)* a dog.

Interjections

5. Marvin scared me when he said, "*(Boo, Gosh)*!"

Next Step: Write a sentence that shows excitement. Use an interjection.

Practice Test

For each underlined word in the following sentences, write the letter that shows what part of speech it is.

1. Kate wrote a <u>poem</u>.
   a. noun   **b.** pronoun   **c.** adverb

2. Are <u>you</u> a student at this school?
   a. noun   **b.** pronoun   **c.** verb

3. The flower <u>bends</u> in the wind.
   a. noun   **b.** verb   **c.** adverb

4. A <u>huge</u> cloud hid the sun.
   a. adjective   **b.** adverb   **c.** noun

5. Robbie stood <u>outside</u>.
   a. adverb   **b.** interjection   **c.** verb

Acknowledgements

We are grateful to many people who helped build the *Write Source* text. First, we must thank all the teachers and students from across the country who contributed ideas and writing models.

Another thanks goes to our team of educators, editors, and designers on our Write Source/Great Source team for all their hard work and dedication to this project.

Steven J. Augustyn, Laura Bachman, Ron Bachman, April Barrons, Colleen Belmont, Evelyn Curley, Chris Erickson, Mark Fairweather, Jean Fischer, Mariellen Hanrahan, Tammy Hintz, Rob King, Lois Krenzke, Mark Lalumondier, Joyce Becker Lee, Ellen Leitheusser, Michele Order Litant, Dian Lynch, Colleen McCarthy, Sheryl Mendicino, Pat Moore, Kevin Nelson, Sue Paro, Pat Reigel, Jason C. Reynolds, Christine Rieker, Susan Rogalski, Chip Rosenthal, Janae Sebranek, Richard Spencer, Julie Spicuzza, Thomas Spicuzza, Stephen D. Sullivan, Jean Varley, and Claire Ziffer.

Credits

Index

The index will help you find specific information in this book. Words that are in italics are from the "Using the Right Word" section. The colored boxes contain information you will use often.